Contents

Dedication		1
Preface		2
Chapter One:	Seasoned Words	5
Chapter Two:	The Temptation	9
Chapter Three:	Overwhelmed and Overcome	19
Chapter Four:	The Dark Years	29
Chapter Five:	The Toll of Homosexuality	37
Chapter Six:	Free At Last	49
Chapter Seven:	Oh No! Not Again!	61
Chapter Eight:	Invincible Love, Part One	69
Chapter Nine:	Invincible Love, Part Two	79
Chapter Ten:	God, The Matchmaker	91

From Her Perspective

Chapter One:	The Beginning of Change	103
Chapter Two:	The Big Revelation	115
Chapter Three:	Free Indeed	121

Conclusion: Heart to Heart	129
Questions and Answers	133
Prayer of Salvation	136

Robert & Kimberly — 21 Years Later: Look What the Lord Has Done!

From Her Perspective	144
From His Perspective	149

Acknowledgements	155
Saving the Best for Last	159
About the Authors	161

OUT OF THE CLOSET
AND INTO
GOD'S LOVE

Robert & Kimberly Pinkney

HARRISHOUSE BOOKS

ALABAMA

Out of the Closet and into GOD'S Love
Written by Robert & Kimberly Pinkney
© 2000 by Robert Pinkney
2nd Edition

Printed and bound in the United States of America. Published by Harris Publishing Company. All rights reserved. No part of this publication may be reproduced or transmitted in any form or by any means, electronic or mechanical, including but not limited to photocopying, recording, or by any information storage and retrieval system, without the written permission from the publisher or the authors.

Harris Publishing Company ISBN:
10 digit: 0976011689   13 digit: 9780976011682

www.harrispubco.com

Printed in the United States of America

www.thesovexperience.org

Dedication

This book is wholeheartedly dedicated to my family, which is a constant reminder of the absolute goodness and ability of God.

To my beautiful, faithful and supportive wife: Kimberly, my capable helpmeet!

To my adorable daughters: Andréya and Brionna.

To my sons: Robert, Jr. (aka Gerald) and Geoffrey

Look what the Lord has done!

Preface

When I was baptized in the fall of 1984, my pastor at the time uttered the following prophecy over me: "The very thing that Satan used to destroy your life, God is going to use to bring glory to His name."

I knew instantly what he was talking about—and not because I had some intimate connection with God. On the contrary, I had been somewhat involved with the devil, and I knew what one thing he had constantly used against me: homosexuality.

What I didn't know, however, was exactly how God would fulfill this particular prophecy. At the time, I was very shy and not all interested in sharing my past of homosexuality with anyone! I was just glad to be free. I didn't know then that I had what it took to get other people free.

As the years passed, however, things gradually began to change. I began to share about my experiences on an individual basis. And though many people were blessed, I chose carefully to whom I revealed the secrets of my past. I certainly was not ready to let the whole world know.

Later, I did realize that someday my story would be in print. However, I was prepared to resist that day as long as possible. I didn't want to become known as the man whom God delivered from homosexuality. I felt surely there is more to me than that. And though I was quite fond of the idea of being published, I thought of many other things about which I could write. Homosexuality was just not tops on that list. Actually, it was not even on the list!

I would, however, eventually become a little bolder about sharing my past. I was able to tell more and more people, but still strictly on an individual basis. Once though, I ventured to share my testimony in its entirety before a church that I attended in San Antonio, Texas. I must admit that things went fairly well, and the people were obviously blessed.

However, things did not go as well during another time when I merely alluded to my past before that same congregation. One of the visitors promptly arose and walked out of the church, never to return. This was difficult for me, as I secretly contemplated if I would ever again dare to share my testimony before a group of people. It didn't matter to me that one woman wept as I shared, obviously touched by the delivering power of God. It mattered less that another lady confided in me later that she had been blessed by my testimony. All I could see was that one person walking out of the church. I let it get to me.

Years after that incident, my wife and I were visiting some old friends of mine. They knew of my testimony, but I shared it regardless as there were some new developments of which they were unaware. My wife also shared with me. At the conclusion of our testimony, it was clear that the Holy Spirit had graced us with His presence. My friends wondered aloud if I would eventually put my story to print. One of them encouraged me, "You certainly have a story to tell." I was certain that I had a story. It was just the telling part with which I was still not comfortable.

Then later, I shared the story with two ladies, neither of which had ever been involved with homosexuality. When I finished, one of them was crying. The other was visibly touched. Again, they urged me to write my story. It was then that I realized that my story was not just a homosexual story. It was a story of triumphing over pain; it was a story of encountering and being permanently transformed by the love of God; it was a story of coming out of bondage into lasting freedom. As such, it was a story for everyone. I resolved to write it, though still not quite at home with the idea.

Finally, I was sitting on my porch one afternoon reading the Bible and praying. Suddenly, a spirit of praise overwhelmed me, to which I yielded. I began to think of the blessings of God, namely my wife and children. I realized that at one time, I utterly despaired of having the life today that I almost took for granted. I also realized that I had no right to withhold a testimony that would ultimately bring great blessings to its hearers. It was in that instance that I pledged obedience to share my testimony of love and deliverance with all who needed to hear.

And so I have resolved here to share this story as best as I remember it. And at last, I am completely at peace with the idea. My wife, Kimberly, has joined me, as the story is as much hers as it is mine. She has added her special touches to it so that you can get a more continuous perspective of what God did for both of us. She also intends to show what it was like to be called to be the wife of someone that was once involved with homosexuality. In so doing, perhaps she can encourage those of you who are faced with the same decision.

My ultimate goal in sharing this story can be summed up in the words of Jesus as recorded in Luke 4:18-19, Amplified: "The Spirit of the Lord is upon Me, because He has anointed Me [the Anointed One, the Messiah] to preach the good news to the poor; He has sent me to announce release to the captives and recovery of sight to the blind, to send forth as delivered those who are oppressed [who are downtrodden, bruised, crushed, and broken down by calamity], to proclaim the acceptable year of the Lord [the day when salvation and the free favors of God profusely abound]." In the light of this scripture, I realize that my story is really His story concerning me. And if you simply trust Him with your life, you will have a similar story of lasting freedom from the proverbial chains that bind.

Prepare to be blessed!

Chapter One

SEASONED WORDS

The first part of Isaiah 50:4 is an awesome scripture, and it appears in its entirety below:

> **"The Lord God hath given me the tongue of the learned, that I should know how to speak a word in season to him that is weary..."**

Our culture today has a tendency to ignore the influence of words upon a person's life. But this scripture is somewhat emphatic in its position that not only are words influential, but also a word spoken in due season especially contains impacting ability. In fact, this scripture further contends that a person who speaks such a word is a person of wisdom. This fact of scripture may not be difficult to understand if you've ever experienced a moment of weariness. Perhaps you have, and if so, do you recall how it felt to have someone say the right thing to you at the right time? Comforting? Encouraging? Empowering? What they said to you were words spoken in season.

In season, according to the dictionary, means "at the right or proper time." In our society where technology evolves faster than the speed of light, it is hard for us to grasp the importance of proper timing. Consider a farmer and how he plants a particular crop during a particular season. The farmer understands a basic principle of sowing and reaping: the season during which he plants is crucial in obtaining the harvest he desires. In other words, if a farmer plants at the right time, he is assured of the harvest when he needs it. This is also the case with speaking a word in season. It may not produce immediately, but if nourished properly, a harvest of blessing is forthcoming. What's more, a word spoken in season will also empower you to endure until the time of harvest. Perhaps, you've plowed through a particularly rough spot in your life because of words you heard during a crisis. Let's face it: words matter!

But if your words—or someone else's words—are so consequential, then how much more are God's words. Can you imagine what it is like to have God speak words to your spirit? Words filled with protection against the destructive intentions of the devil for your life. Words that for years would repeatedly rescue you from the depths of despair. That would offer you life and then enable you to accept that life when all you want to do is die. Words that would buoy you, time after time, with courage and hope when fear and pain obscure every experience in your life. My friend, these are words spoken in season. And I don't have to imagine what they are like because I've been wonderfully privileged to hear them at many times in my life. Crude as this may sound, they are alive and capable of reproduction in much the same way (perhaps more!) as the union of a sperm and an egg.

I remember one particular occasion when God spoke such words to me even though it was such a long time ago. I cannot recall my exact age; however, I could not have been more than six years old because I had not yet begun first grade. I don't remember the day of the week, or what the weather was like, or what I was wearing, or even what I had for dinner that day. I don't even remember what time of day it was. But I do remember emphatically that God spoke to me. And I will never forget what He said: "you will be a husband, a father and a preacher." What a momentous promise when you consider that at the time, I didn't know what a husband was, did not know where babies came from, and did not have a clue about the provision of the new birth.

And yet, God has fulfilled every part of this word in my life. Psalms 37:23 reveals that the Lord delights or is interested in our way, making sure that we choose the way that is right so we can enjoy the life that is right (see John 10:10). How wonderful for me to have been of importance to God when I was just a young child, when I had absolutely nothing to offer. But then again, we could never merit God's words of blessing, which incidentally are always spoken in season. This fact is borne out over and over throughout the Bible. Sarah was controlled by unbelief when confronted with angelic tidings of Isaac's impending birth. Gideon was cowering in fear when the Lord summoned him with "seasoned" words to deliver Israel from the bondage of the Midianites. The widow woman of Zarephath was preparing to die when God, through Elijah, spoke victory into her situation. Paul was involved in strategic genocide—of the Christian race!—when God called him to evangelize the Gentiles with the gospel that he had so vehemently opposed. Need I say more?

At this point, you might wonder how I, being so young, was able to discern the voice of God. If the truth were told, I actually did not realize at the time that God was speaking to me. You must understand that I did not hear God as Samuel did in the Old Testament. There was no audible voice, and definitely no "Eli" to point out to me that it was indeed God speaking to me. There was simply a knowing on the inside, quiet unassuming words coursing gently through my very being. And when it was over, I simply knew that someday, I would be a husband, a father and a preacher. But it would be years before I would eventually come to realize that those fateful words were simply God's way of allowing me a small peek into His vast plan for my life, a plan that He

is even now implementing and unraveling. But at the time, I simply chalked it up to a dream of mine, sort of the answer to the proverbial question: *what do you want to be when you grow up?* How could I have known that those would be the very words that would one day save my life?

Chapter Two

THE TEMPTATION

In retrospect, I realize that God not only spoke to me, but His timing was also absolutely impeccable. Shortly after my encounter with God, I would face a temptation that was beyond my ability to resist. It would be the beginning of many long years of a dark struggle that would eventually threaten my sanity and even my life. But before I get to that, I need to do a brief Biblical study highlighting the importance of a word from God. You see: I am thoroughly convinced that if I had not heard words from God as a young lad, I would not have made it through that dark time to which I've just alluded. In fact, I know I would be dead by now and perhaps in hell. I so want you to know that God also has words for you that will bring you completely out of any bondage to which you are subjected.

The fourth chapter of the book of Mark contains the parable of the sower. This parable reveals that there are four types of grounds upon which the Word of God can be sown: by the way side, on stony ground, among thorns and on good ground. In every case except the last, the sowing of the word did not result in a harvest. Jesus explains why the other grounds failed to yield a harvest, and certainly His explanation is noteworthy, but it is not my focus at this time. What I am interested in, however, is the fourth ground. Consider the following scripture:

> **"And others fell on good ground, and did yield fruit that sprang up and increased; and brought forth, some thirty, and some sixty, and some hundred" (Mark 4:8).**

There are many worthwhile things that can be said about this scripture, but what I want to point out is that this ground received a harvest. So what this indicates to me is that God's Word spoken in season is always—underline "always"—meant to produce a harvest. When God speaks words to you, He is not merely trying to encourage or strengthen you. Doubtlessly, His words will bring encouragement and strength. But most importantly, what God speaks He absolutely will fulfill. In fact, this is exactly the reason He speaks: to bring fulfillment in your life of all that is good and profitable. And sometimes, that may mean speaking a word for the specific purpose of terminating the evil in your life that stands against God's good plans for you (See Jeremiah 29:11). Consider also Numbers 23:19, "God is not a man that He should lie, neither the son of man that He should repent: hath He said, and shall He not do it? Or hath He spoken, and shall He not make it good?"

One other thing I've learned over the years: God is just as interested in speaking to sinners as He is in speaking to Christians. In fact, His compassion for sinners is unfathomable. Jesus Himself said, "I am not come to call the righteous, but sinners to repentance" (Matt. 9:13b). Does this not make perfect sense when you think about it? What man, because of his righteousness, summoned Jesus out of heaven to shed His righteous blood? According to the Bible, there was absolutely none (Rom. 3:10). God didn't send Jesus out of heaven to die a humiliating death on the cross because the world was full of righteous people. Au contraire! He sent Jesus because the world was sinful and in dire need of a Savior.

So if you are a sinner who happens to be reading this book, I can make you one guarantee. As you read, God will speak to you. If you listen and believe, you too can be free. So please, I implore you, continue reading. Don't let your sin stop you; it didn't stop God. Somehow, I know you want to be free.

Let us continue with the story. As I was saying, not long after God spoke to me words in season, I was confronted by a dark temptation. I began to have thoughts and feelings of homosexuality. I had no idea at the time that this was simply a manifestation of a demon of homosexuality trying to gain access to my soul. For the feelings and thoughts seemed very much to be my own. I remember that as I would sit and watch steamy love scenes on television, I would literally feel sexual emotions stirring on the inside of me. I might not have otherwise been alarmed, but I realized almost immediately that invariably, the male participant in the love scene was arousing the emotions I felt. To complicate matters, I knew beyond the shadow of a doubt that what I was feeling was wrong. Now no one ever told me that. I was not yet literate, so I had not learned it from reading. I knew very little if anything about Christian morals. But somehow, down on the inside of me, I just knew that homosexuality was something to be shunned. Unfortunately, I didn't know how to do that.

When I was first confronted with temptations of homosexuality, I was still very young. At the time of this writing, my oldest child is a little over half past six years old. It seems almost unreal to me, as I am sure it does to most parents, that the devil would actually tempt my child in the way that he tempted me. But cold reality sets in as I remember that I could not have been much older then than she is now when temptation initially crossed my path.

Of course, I realize now that the atmosphere in which I was raised was conducive to temptation. Although my parents were regular churchgoers, they did not understand how to counter demonic activity in their home. They didn't adequately monitor what we watched on the tube. In their defense, however, I must admit: who would have thought that a televised sex scene—tamed by today's standards—would have ignited such strong sexual feelings in a child? But they also did not share the gospel with me. So then, when the enemy came, I had absolutely no defense. Furthermore, they did not know how to seek God concerning their children. So they had no idea that I was beginning what would prove to be one of the greatest storms in my life. And oh how bitterly I would be tossed before the storm was over.

I certainly hope that I have the attention of some parent right now. I would urge you unashamedly to commit wholeheartedly to the spiritual nurturing of your children. Make sure they are consistently exposed to the Word of God. Pray for and with them. Teach them how to recognize and stand against the wiles of the devil. Instill in them a love and longing for the things of God. Do it while they are little! I do not advise you as a parent, but as someone that, as a young child, and then as a teenager, was so completely devastated by sin's vile dominion that more than once, I lost the resolve to live.

Oh how children need godly, fearless, demon-defying parents that will adamantly oppose every foul plan of Satan against their children. One thing you absolutely must understand: the devil is definitely interested in your children. His desire is to gain access to them while they are very young and steal the plan of prosperity and peace that God has in store for them. How persistently he works to accomplish his evil purpose. And often, he is successful for far too long. It is wonderful that we serve a God who can and will skillfully undo any havoc that the devil may have wreaked in our lives. But how much greater it would be to have covenant-conscious parents who deny the devil the access to their children that he so relentlessly seeks! The good news is that God is interested in our children and has a plan for them (Jeremiah 29:11). He has provided an impregnable network of children and youth ministries that make raising godly children almost a foregone conclusion.

Actually, today there is very little reason for a child to be overtaken by temptation as I was—that is, if parents avail themselves of the available resources for raising godly children. My point is that children will always be tempted, even in greatest of environments, but they never have to be overwhelmed. The fact remains, however, that I did face the dark demon of homosexuality. In retrospect, I realize that for me, it was a lost cause from the very beginning. At first, I tried to pretend that nothing was happening. But as the feelings got stronger, ignoring them became less of a viable option. And then I resolved to resist them. I knew they were wrong, and so I decided that I simply would not give in to them.

I believe now that resisting homosexuality was indeed the right thing to do. In fact, James 4:7 instructs us to do this very thing: "Resist the devil and he will flee." The way I chose to resist, however, was the problem. The scripture that instructs us to resist the devil also instructs us to submit to God. Therefore, you cannot successfully resist the devil until you submit to God. And submitting to God means submitting to His Word. So then, the way we resist temptation is by submitting to the Word of God. As a little boy, I didn't know how to resist my homosexual proclivities. I just knew they had to be resisted. And so with my will alone, I tried to resist one of the greatest temptations that I have ever faced in my life! And I do not exaggerate: I have faced many dark times in my life, but none darker than my battle with homosexuality!

Years later while caught helplessly in the throes of homosexuality, I was sure God had forsaken me. Sometimes, I was even bitter. Why had God let this happen to me? Of course now, I realize that God was not the problem. The problem was I! And one thing you can be sure of is that God is not the problem in your situation either. Looking back, I can see things more clearly. As a child when I encountered this temptation, I was unsaved and ignorant concerning the things of God. God has a kingdom, a specific way of operating, and if we want God's help in our situations, then we must conform to His specific way of operating. Ignorance is no excuse, and contrary to popular opinion, what you don't know can hurt you. Nevertheless, God will do all that He can to bring revelation so that a person can operate in His kingdom and get results.

When God wanted to create light, He spoke it into existence. When God wanted to create the earth, He spoke it into existence. When God wanted to create man, He spoke it and then formed him into existence. When God wanted to make Abram a father of nations, not only did He speak it but He also changed his name to Abraham so that Abraham would speak it also. And most importantly, when God saw that humanity would surely die and spend eternity in hell without the intervention of a Savior, what did He do? He prophesied a Savior through all the prophets, over and over, until Jesus stood erected, bloody and beaten, on a cross remitting forever the sins of all humanity. I am trying to show you that spoken words carry weight with God.

If we want freedom from bad situations, then we must speak God's words. And so I finally got to the place where I understood something very crucial. When God told me as a little boy that I would be a husband, a father and a preacher, He was giving me everything I needed to put down the temptation of homosexuality. And to top it off, God got to me before the devil came with his temptation.

When the devil showed up, I should have resisted him with the words God gave me: "No devil. God has already told me that I am to be a husband, a father and a preacher. This means that I cannot be a homosexual. So I refuse your offer." I should have said this every time until the devil concluded that there was no use tempting me with homosexuality. This has worked for me many times and with various situations since I became a Christian.

Well, you know what they say about hindsight being 20/20. At the time, I didn't know how to resist temptation. And so I endeavored to use will power. Of course, this did not involve speaking. I simply tried to push the thoughts out of my mind. The only external manifestation of my internal struggle was an occasional grimace when I tried especially hard to resist the feelings. As time passed, however, my feelings would become more difficult to resist. Despite all my efforts, the temptation persisted and actually increased in frequency and intensity.

Oh, I thought, *if I only had someone to talk to*. Certainly, someone understood my predicament and could help me. But there was no one. And if there were, I was too afraid to speak out. I knew at the time that homosexuality was not an acceptable form of behavior in society, and definitely not in my family. I had three older brothers, and none of them seemed to be indicating the tendencies with which I struggled. And even though I had not yet committed any acts of homosexuality, I was ashamed. Ashamed of the way I felt. Ashamed of the thoughts that constantly plagued my mind; thoughts that were beginning to form a very dangerous imagination. I was utterly ashamed that I was a boy who wanted to be a girl. And so how could I possibly breathe a word of my struggle to anyone?

I shuddered at the very thought of anyone ever discovering what was going on with me. I was determined that I would beat this. But the harder I tried the stronger the thoughts and feelings became. Clearly, the devil was as determined as I, perhaps even more so. I found myself thinking about guys all the time. Thinking back, I am almost incredulous. I mean I was a child—a child!—struggling with adult- sized emotions. Think of it: I was a little boy trying desperately not to succumb to homosexuality. It just seems that a little boy should not be faced with such a monumental temptation. But the sad fact is that the devil goes after children. Your little son, or grandson, or nephew, or cousin, or your friend's son may be going through exactly the same thing. But I digress.

As I said, the harder I tried to resist the harder resistance became. Eventually, my plight would extend beyond just mere feelings. I found that I could identify more easily with girls, and for this reason preferred to play with girls. At home, though I spent time in play with my brothers, my sister was my primary playmate and playing with dolls was one of my favorite pastimes. I didn't like doing any of the things boys did. I didn't like playing with trucks. I didn't like girls, at least not in the traditional romantic sense. And so I didn't like spending time with boys talking about girls. And I abhorred football.

The struggle would soon be elevated to involve my mannerisms, as they became increasingly feminine. I walked like a girl, stood like a girl, flipped my hands like a girl, and crossed my legs like a girl. I incorporated the female language—and yes, there is one—into my vocabulary. In short, I talked like a girl. It seemed that the demon of homosexuality had already gained access to my soul and was confidently waiting for the day when I would seal my doom with a homosexual act: and all this before I was finished with elementary school.

To my peers, friends and family, my feminine mannerisms became evidence that I was either homosexual or heading that way fast. People, especially boys, began to ostracize me. I was teased often and constantly assailed with demeaning names, such as *sissy*, *faggot* and *punk*. I quickly realized that not only did I have to fight feelings of homosexuality, but I also had to hide those feelings from everyone. I learned to pretend and deny what I was experiencing. But I was hardly able to deceive anyone. As time passed, the feelings would become stronger, my mannerisms more exaggerated and my peers more suspicious of my behavior. The name-calling became more frequent, and I became more and more ashamed. More than once, I wished that somebody somewhere would come and put an end to my torment. And perhaps, there was someone. Perhaps, I was just too embarrassed to inquire.

Even I was beginning to realize that the battle was too great for me. The devil was fast destroying every defense that I put up. I was running scared! What would become of me? How could I go on resisting the feelings that raged in me like boiling water under cover? Yet how could I give into them? Oh if only homosexuality was a socially acceptable behavior, then I could come to terms with it. I could throw caution to the wind and explore these feelings that just wouldn't go away. I could stand up and be homosexual and proud.

But deep down inside, I knew this wasn't true. I understood all too well that it was not public disdain alone that kept me from embracing homosexuality. It was years before I would read in the first chapter of Romans God's take on homosexuality. It was years before I would read the account of the judgment of Sodom and Gomorrah or before I heard any preacher lambaste homosexuality. But somehow, I knew, from the onset of my struggle, that homosexuality is a sin and brings displeasure to God. And even though I wasn't saved—didn't even know how to get saved—I loved God and didn't want to displease Him.

Now I know that some of you find it difficult to believe that I actually loved God in my condition. Not only did I love Him then, but also years later when I was fully involved with homosexuality, I still loved God. What you fail to realize is that there are multitudes of sinners that love God. They are confused and do not understand why they do the things they do. Consider the following verses of scripture:

> **For I know that in me (that is, in my flesh,) dwelleth no good thing: for to will is present with me, but how to perform that which is good I find not. For the good I would I do not; but the evil which I would not, that I do...when I would do good, evil is present with me (Rom. 7:18, 19, 21).**

I understand here that Paul is speaking of the Christian who has not fully committed himself to Christ. But believe me, this scripture also describes the plight of many sinners. A sinner especially has not experienced the empowerment of the new birth. So when his flesh, which contains no good thing, makes a demand, he has no choice but to grant it. He does not possess the power of resistance like the Christian does. He can only resist from his will, and he certainly may for a time, but sheer will power, no matter how strong, is never enough to thwart the advances of the devil. So it is not at all unusual for a sinner to find himself repeatedly doing things that he knows are wrong and that he does not want to do. So many times, we as Christians lose sight of this fact. And so instead of attracting people with empathy and compassion, we often repel them with our judgmental and self-righteous attitudes.

At any rate, I was just like the person described in the scripture above. I recognized the homosexual tendencies within me to be evil, but I was having very little success resisting them. It seemed, with each passing day, that I was becoming more wearied by the struggle within me. It seemed indeed that surrendering to my feelings was inevitable. I did not know if I could last. I was running scared!

Chapter Three

OVERWHELMED AND OVERCOME

II Corinthians 10:4, 5 outlines a principle that if followed can bring victory to every situation every time.

> **For the weapons of our warfare are not carnal, but mighty through God to the pulling down of strongholds; Casting down imaginations and every high thing that exalts itself against the knowledge of God, and bringing into captivity every thought to the obedience of Christ.**

One of the first things that you must realize is that you are involved in warfare. Now that warfare may involve homosexuality, drug addiction or any number of bondages. But the fact remains that you are involved in warfare. And Ephesians 6:12 reveals the source of that warfare:

> **We wrestle not against flesh and blood, but against principalities, against powers, against the rulers of the darkness of this world, against spiritual wickedness in high places.**

Principalities, powers, rulers of darkness and spiritual wickedness are all levels of demonic authority. So regardless of your position, if you're involved in a fight—and who among us is not—then your fight is against demonic authority. Please understand that the devil does not reserve his opposition for Christians only. Don't think you are safe from his attacks because you are a sinner. The devil will stand against anyone who has the audacity to desire anything other than what he has to offer. You don't have to be a Christian to be the object of his disgust.

Now if you are anything like I was, then you know this already. I was confused, embittered, driven and tossed uncontrollably in my emotions. I wasn't taught about demonic activity. But I knew unmistakably that there was something on the inside of me working in direct opposition to what I knew to be right. Something incredibly determined to drive me to commit acts I abhorred and knew to be wrong. You know, when you think about it, the devil is not really that hard to spot, is he? My problem, however, was I didn't know how to fight. I didn't know how to silence the demon within. In fact, he could not be silenced. He had to be dethroned, and I certainly did not know how to do that.

This brings me to the second point of this scripture. You must realize that we don't fight with carnal weapons. The dictionary defines carnal as *worldly, secular or unspiritual*. Now that you understand where your attack originates, let me ask you this question. How can you upend a spiritual attack with an unspiritual weapon?

Paul once referred to the Corinthians as carnal. The word translated carnal is the Greek word *sarkikos*. It refers to someone who is without the power of God, without the advantage of His presence. So then when we try to fight a spirit-induced war with carnal weapons, we are fighting without the power of God and without the advantage of His presence. Without God, there is absolutely no hope or guarantee of victory. Unbeknownst to me, this is exactly how I tried to resist the temptation of homosexuality. I used my will power, a carnal weapon, to fight off his attacks. But the more I resisted, the more persistent the thoughts and feelings became. Why? Because in my attempt to fight a spiritual war with carnal weapons, without the power or presence of

God, I had absolutely no effect on the devil. He simply regrouped and came against me with even greater force.

The only thing I managed to do was to wear myself out while still years away from the victory I so desperately needed. So then resisting without the presence or power of God was my first mistake.

Now that you know how to resist, what exactly are you resisting? According to II Corinthians 10:4, you should be pulling down strongholds. One of the synonyms for *stronghold* is *fortress*. A fortress is a place built with walls and defenses. Keep this definition in mind, as it will come into play shortly. It is imperative that we understand that our position in the fight is to pull down strongholds or fortresses. That is what we do. That is how we win.

It now becomes necessary to ask what and where are these strongholds we are supposed to be pulling down? II Corinthians 10:5 answers this question:

> **Casting down imaginations, and every high thing that exalteth itself against the knowledge of God, and bringing into captivity every thought to the obedience of Christ.**

The strongholds (or fortresses) that we are to pull down are imaginations and thoughts. These thoughts and ideas are in your mind; therefore, the strongholds are in your mind. Remember the definition for fortress? Well, what the devil has done over a period of time is influenced your mind with his thoughts and ideas. Once you embrace his ideas and thoughts, he erects fortresses, or walls of defenses, to keep his thoughts in and God's thoughts out. However, Paul in Romans 12:2 provides the key to destroying the devil's fortresses. He admonishes us to renew our minds. Then again, in Ephesians 5:26, Paul uses the phrase *washing of water by the word*. In doing so, he assigns a washing or purifying property to the Word of God. When we put these two scriptures together, we come to a clear understanding of how we are to renew our minds. We do so by replacing the devil's ideas with God's ideas, which we get from the Bible. And this, my friend, is when the battle is most heated.

It is crucial to realize that imaginations should be treated differently from thoughts. The same passage of scripture that instructs us to cast down imaginations simply requires us to bring thoughts subject to the obedience of Christ. There is good reason for this. A thought is an imagination in seedling form. In other words, if a thought, whether good or bad, is allowed to persist in the mind, it will eventually become an imagination. As such, an evil thought is not as advanced as an evil imagination; however, it needs to be replaced before forming an evil imagination. A good thought is a thought that is already subject to the obedience of Christ. A bad thought must become subject. For instance, when the devil first tempted me with homosexuality, it was merely a thought or feeling. As such, I should have made it subject to the obedience of Christ. For me, the obedience of Christ would have been the word in season that God had already spoken to me: *you will be a husband, a father and a preacher*.

How exactly do you bring a thought into captivity? In order to answer that question, I must impose on you to participate in a little exercise for me. In your mind, begin counting from one to ten. One…two…three…four… Now say **Jesus** out loud. In order to say **Jesus**, you had to stop counting, didn't you? You may have gotten distracted trying to follow my instructions. So try the exercise again. Do it as many times as you'd like. You will always come to the same conclusion: in order to say **Jesus** out loud, you have to stop counting in your mind. You see, a word spoken with the mouth take precedence over a thought in the mind. And this is exactly how you bring a thought into captivity. You speak to it. You don't try to ignore it. You don't try to shrug it off. You speak to it. When thoughts of homosexuality first entered my mind, I should have spoken against them, using the words that God had spoken to me. Instead, I tried to will them away.

Now that we know how to deal with evil thoughts, let's examine this subject a little further. Why are we instructed to cast down imaginations? Why not rather bring them into subjection as well? According to the dictionary, an imagination involves the power to create (in the mind) believable or realistic pictures of things not present to the senses. An evil imagination is a buildup of thoughts that have not been brought captive to the obedience of Christ. Although the imagination consists of things not yet present to the senses, it is through the imagination that these things not yet present to the senses become a reality. So then, the imagination is the last step before manifestation. All the things that you are able to see—great architecture, great financial empires, great accomplishments and even this great country—are products of someone's imagination.

When you see the imagination from this perspective, then you can readily understand why you should deal with an evil imagination more drastically than an evil thought. An imagination is far more advanced and far more dangerous than a mere thought.

An evil imagination is not just a buildup of evil thoughts, but of evil thoughts in revolution or rebellion. As such, it must be cast down. Consider the following analogy.

Once upon a time, a group of English colonists, for a number of reasons, grew disgruntled with English rule. Eventually, they decided to start what we know today as the American Revolution. Before the revolution, the colonists expressed their discontent with British rule in a number of ways. However, they were not yet interested in staging a full-scale rebellion. At this point, you could say that their discontent was in the *thought* phase. By the time of the war, however, the colonists' discontent had grown to the point where they were determined to take whatever action necessary to gain their freedom from British rule. Their discontent had reached the *imagination* stage. At this point, Britain's only recourse was to attempt a putdown of the colonists' rebellion.

Any other action would have all but guaranteed the establishment of America. Fortunately, the British were unsuccessful in their attempt to stop the colonists.

In keeping with this analogy, an evil imagination is a rebellion; for the Bible says it "exalteth itself against the knowledge of God." And as a rebellion, it must be put down. It cannot be reasoned with; it cannot be explained away, and it will not be ignored. If left unchecked, an imagination will become a reality.

In my battle against the temptation of homosexuality, I would finally reach the place where I would no longer just be dealing with thoughts. The temptation was beginning to affect my imagination. It took a few years; nevertheless, it still happened. I would begin to see pictures in my mind of the acts of homosexuality. Aided by the love scenes I saw on television, I could clearly imagine what it would be like to have sex with another man. With the imagination came stronger feelings and a very real fear that I wouldn't be able to resist much longer.

My fears were justified. The devil was moving in for the kill. Pictures of homosexual acts plagued my mind constantly. And I was not casting them down. In fact, I was horrified. I cringed each time the devil brought a picture before my mind. And fear of these pictures seemed to act as a catalyst for their frequent occurrence. I knew that it would only be a matter of time before I could resist no longer. I was as frightened as a prey before its predator, a victim before its assailant. But still I fought, hoping against hope that I could somehow exorcise this demon from my soul. In the end, I would prove too weak for the challenge—all my strength extinguished by the burden of guilt and shame, and overpowered by the constant onslaught of feelings now accompanied by a very lively imagination. I would cry out to God, but not out of faith, not really believing that He could do anything for me. *Oh God, please help me. I can't fight these feelings anymore. I don't want to do what I am thinking of doing.*

The day would arrive when I, like Job, would curse the day I was born. No meteorologist alive could have predicted how dark the day would be. Oh sure, it was perhaps a bright shiny day, but the darkness that pervaded my soul was somehow able to overshadow the day as well. I met a guy who was three years my senior. He was a relative of a very close friend of my family. When he made sexual advances towards me, at first I tried to resist. However, I was not prepared for the feelings that ensued. My feelings, cooped up and denied for so long, went through the proverbial roof. Before I knew it, I had done the inevitable, the irrevocable, and as far as I was concerned, the unforgivable.

How utterly devastated I was! The devil had succeeded in getting me to do what I had fought so hard and so long not to do. And he accomplished this in just the way that I've outlined in this chapter. First, he came to me with thoughts of homosexuality that I failed to bring captive to the obedience of Christ. These thoughts persisted and built up over a period of time. Then the devil began to build my imagination with pictures of homosexuality. Because I did not cast down the imagination, I had no choice but to succumb to it. Yes, the devil had won. And I was only eleven. I mention my age here because I want you to understand how ruthless, how utterly disrespecting, the devil is when it comes to implementing his dark plans for humanity. He has no qualms about enslaving children to his dastardly desires.

I talked myself into believing that I would only do it once. I was determined to keep this from happening again. Somehow, I thought that if I could walk the straight and narrow from now on, God would be able to overlook this isolated episode of sin. Yeah, that's what I would do. I would fight hard to keep the demon of homosexuality from expressing itself again. I had waged this battle successfully for years. Surely, I could do it again. But when the opportunity presented itself again, my resolve was not as strong as before. I actually yielded to the temptation with greater ease. And with each new temptation, the yielding would become easier, almost automatic. The devil had me firmly under his grasp.

I was chagrined. What was I going to do now? That I was clearly involved in homosexuality I could no longer deny. But I was still afraid. Afraid of what my family would think. Afraid of what my friends would think. And I was petrified that I had committed the unpardonable sin. Besides, I was still not sold on this idea of homosexuality. It was then that I decided to keep this part of my life a secret. Absolutely no one must know! And so, for me, began a secret life of sheer hell.

I have often heard of guys who were adults before discovering a penchant for homosexuality, but I can't relate to this at all. In fact, I frankly find it hard to believe because I was barely school age when I became aware of feelings that courted homosexuality. And I was barely in middle school when I gave expression to those feelings. Other men can pinpoint a bad experience, such as sexual molestation, that started them down the road towards sexual perversion. I am more inclined to believe them; however, this is not my story. I was never molested. And certainly, no one tried to sway me. In fact, all the people I met made it clear that they were adamantly opposed to homosexuality. This is one of the reasons that I was so ashamed and found it extremely difficult to share my feelings with anyone.

My story is—and I am convinced that this is the story of most men and women caught in the clutches of homosexuality—that I was simply assailed by overwhelming feelings when I was but a small child. This is how it all began. Many men and women are hopelessly convinced that homosexuality is God's will for their lives. They contend that their homosexual orientation is simply a fact of their birth. They believe this because at a very young age, they were confronted with feelings of homosexuality. Because of this, they don't remember feeling any other way. In fact, most of them have never felt anything but homosexual. And they have felt homosexual as long as a heterosexual has felt heterosexual. So naturally, they conclude that they were meant to be homosexual.

Even scientists have jumped on this bandwagon claiming to have discovered genes that are "directed" for homosexuality. But what people fail to realize is that genetics don't reveal God's intent for a person. Genes simply pass down biological information from one generation to the next. So then, a scientist can never tell me that God intended for me to be a homosexual.

Clearly then, I do not buy into the notion that God's will for me, or anyone for that matter, is homosexuality. However, I will take the controversial stance that perhaps, some people are born with an affinity for homosexuality. Before you dismiss this perspective, let's consider a scripture together:

"Behold, I was shapen in iniquity; and in sin did my mother conceive me" (Psalm 51:5).

While David was king of Israel, he had an adulterous affair with Bathsheba while her husband, Uriah, was away at war. To cover his sin, David had Uriah killed in battle, and then took Bathsheba to be his wife. David's scheme was a secret to everyone except God. God sent to David a prophet by the name of

Nathan to confront him. After the confrontation, David repented and penned Psalm 51. In the fifth verse of this psalm, David, the adulterer, liar and murderer, credits his propensity for sin with being a fact of his birth. He emphatically states, "I was shapen in iniquity [and] in sin did my mother conceive me." In essence, he contends that he was born a sinner. Oddly enough, this is a point with which most homosexuals would agree, especially now that they are allegedly armed with scientific evidence.

But David takes this issue further than science is willing. David understands that his state of birth, or so-called genetic make-up, does not determine what is right or wrong. He also realizes that he needs to undergo some type of change so that he can conform to God's way, which is the right way. He pleads with God to make such a change:

(v.7) Purge me with hyssop, and I shall be clean: wash me, and I shall be whiter than snow. (And v.10) Create in me a clean heart, O God; and renew a right spirit within me.

In other words, regardless of what he believed about his birth, David made a decision first to agree with God's ideas of right and wrong and secondly to do whatever it took to conform to those ideas.

I know all too well that there are some homosexuals that have absolutely no tolerance for what I am saying. You believe that I am narrow-minded, bigoted and a purveyor of hate. Unfortunately, there is very little that I can do for you. Understand though that I used to be a homosexual, and I know what I am talking about. However, I also know that there are a countless number of men and women trapped in homosexuality who are practically begging to be free. I know you are out there, for I've been there myself. You are miserable, ashamed and self-loathing. You can't stand to live another minute in your current state. If that describes you, then you are the person in whom I am interested. You are the reason I write this book.

If you are longing to be free from homosexuality, I can definitely assure you that freedom is available, freedom that is glorious and permanent. But you must come to the same conclusion as David. As you continue to read this book, open up your heart to the freedom that is available for you through Christ. Forget what science says about the way you were genetically engineered. Agree with God that homosexuality is an abominable sin. And then understand that God has provided a way out for you!

Chapter Four

THE DARK YEARS

Like Adam and Eve, I had fallen prey to the devil's schemes. I was certain that my fate of doom was sealed forever. How could God ever forgive me? How could I ever forgive myself? It would be years before I could even fathom that God even cared about me, let alone would forgive me.

I was confused, as I could not understand how I, a mere child, had come to the place where I had committed the most shameful act imaginable. I wasn't confused about homosexuality, however. I knew that I neither now nor ever want to be one! Down on the inside of me, I was very bothered by the whole idea. For all my reasoning, it just did not seem right to me. Before, I had fought against the barrage of thoughts that would routinely assail my mind. Now that the thoughts had given birth to action, I was determined that each act would be my last. This was a tougher fight indeed. Try as I might, I just could not abdicate the demon of homosexuality from the throne of my life.

I fought truculently, my family and friends completely oblivious to the struggle that threatened to rip apart my life. I became even more ashamed and therefore afraid to let others know what was going on with me. This is another one of the devil's tactics. After bringing you into the bondage of sin, he seeks to control you with fear and shame. This way, he can keep you from seeking and obtaining necessary help and counsel from other people.

I lived a most miserable and wretched existence. I was involved in an activity that brought me abject displeasure, and yet I could not stop my involvement. I would often describe myself as a guy with a girl locked up on the inside of me, a girl that absolutely craved expression. And far too often, she would get her way. In fact, homosexuality actually became my master. Countless times, the urge would overshadow me, and I would find myself driven, like a slave to the auction block, to be sold to the vile affection of homosexuality. In short, I could never say no! Can you imagine this: a life of always being compelled to do what you utterly detest? My constant heart cry echoed that of the Apostle Paul:

O wretched man that I am! Who shall deliver me from the body of this death? (Romans 7:24)

It was indeed a form of death that I discovered to be inescapable.

For me, one of the biggest challenges of homosexuality centered on people and how they treated me. For the most part, people rejected me. Even though I tried hard to hide my bent towards homosexuality, my feminine mannerisms always betrayed me. People almost always judge by what they see. And even though looks are often deceptive, in my case, they couldn't have been more telling. So when people saw me (especially other guys) they saw a despicable little punk with whom they wanted nothing to do. They would avoid me like the plague! I have not come to judge the validity of their actions but simply to say, right or wrong, they only served to compound the hurt that already so disoriented my emotions.

I have always been fond of people and during those days, I cared far too much for their opinions of me. So when they rejected me, I would do everything in my power to win their approval. I don't have to tell you what a disaster that turned out to be. I began to consider others to be much better than myself, not in deference to any Biblical mandate, but out of an exaggerated sense of self-hatred. I would begin to do things, or not do things, based on how I thought others would react. This was a double whammy, for not only was homosexuality in control of my life, but I had added a secondary ruler: people and their fluctuating perceptions of who and how I should be. Consequently, there was no place for God in my life. And so I plummeted further into homosexuality.

I must confess, however, that there were some good people in my life that had a genuine regard for my well-being. They recognized my bout with homosexuality and felt it their duty to place me on the right path. I remember one such person, again a family friend and much older than myself. One day while visiting our home, he took me aside and reprimanded me for being a "faggot" and sternly advised me to get my act together. His expression was set like stone, his eyes registering piercing disapproval. He took the hard-line approach, supposing that a little toughness might straighten me out. I simply reverted further into my shell of denial.

Though I did not concede to my friend's admonition, I would later privately ponder his words. Oh how I wanted to end this terror in my life! I wanted to run to my friend and say, "Oh yes, you are right. I am a homosexual. But I do not want to be. Can you please help me?" But I couldn't. I was just too ashamed. Oh I would often cry out to God in desperation and unbelief. *How much longer can I stand this? Will it ever end?*

And then there was a different type of people altogether. Allow me to explain. I had been a practicing homosexual for a little over a year when I met someone who was later to become a good friend. We met in middle school, and shortly after we made acquaintance, he took me into his confidence. He informed me that he was a homosexual. Routinely, he described in detail his sexual escapades. I was shocked, but certainly not because I was innocent. I was simply amazed that he could so easily reveal his homosexual identity to another person. I did finally realize that he only took me into his confidence because he strongly suspected that I was involved in homosexuality as well. So the risk of personal disclosure was minimal. Still, it would take me two years to admit to him what he had known all along, that I too was a homosexual.

One other thing surprised me about my new friend. He seemed to be at peace with homosexuality. Missing in his eyes was the trace of inner turmoil that had come to characterize my very existence. Though he was not officially "out of the closet," he had certainly come to terms with homosexuality. Like so many others, he felt as though it was his unchangeable lot in life. And so he had simply acquiesced and, unlike me, was not bothered by inward strife. When he spoke of homosexuality, he smiled and laughed, like a child enjoying the simple pleasures of life. It seemed that he had found the freedom that had consistently eluded me.

Oh how I wished I could be like him: so peaceful, so happy and so carefree. But I was not willing to pay the price. I was not willing to surrender totally to homosexuality. I couldn't. Something inside of me just wouldn't allow it. As time passed, I would find that there were many other people just like my friend.

In fact, I did not meet even one homosexual that was as tormented as I. I became confused as I began to wonder if I was indeed the dysfunctional one. Perhaps, I was making too big of a deal out of this. Perhaps, I was only experiencing a classic case of denial. But try as I might, I simply could not shake my desire to be free from homosexuality.

We were in high school by now and one day, my friend said to me, "you will never be happy until you realize and accept the fact that you were born to be a homosexual." Without thinking, I responded, "then I will never be happy."

Because of my displeasure with homosexuality, I began early to seek a way out. My search inevitably led me to church. I believed in God, and my parents were avid churchgoers. So attending church easily became a natural activity for me. I came to church, however, armed with half-truths about God. Specifically, I knew He hated sin, but I had no idea that He had already provided a way of escape for anyone caught in sin. I knew nothing of the new birth available through Christ Jesus. I didn't know that I could change. In fact, I was told that I was destined to be a sinner forever. The same people that fed me this line of garbage also shunned me for being a homosexual. What a paradox! It might be funny if it were not so painful.

But erroneous church dogma did not completely deter me from my ambitions of freedom. Hope still lingered in my heart. The words of God still burned, though less brightly, in my spirit: "you will be a husband, a father and a preacher." There just had to be a way out. So I was involved in a continual press towards freedom. Of course, I was going about it the wrong way, but in my heart, I was fighting to be free!

Once, an evangelist came to visit our small town to hold a revival meeting. He was almost finished when I heard about it. I heard a lot of good reports, but what I mainly heard was that people were "catching the Holy Ghost." In my small, religious hometown, "catching the Holy Ghost" was a term primarily used among Black congregants. It simply meant that people were jumping, dancing and shouting praises to God. When I heard about this, I resolved that I wanted to go and be a part of this. Before I went however, I prayed and ask the Lord to let me "catch the Holy Ghost." I know you are probably wondering who this Holy Ghost was and why was He on the run. But this really was a phrase we used during those days.

At any rate, I had never caught the Holy Ghost before, and I thought that if I could just catch the Holy Ghost, maybe I wouldn't have to be a homosexual anymore. I went to service that night nervous but fully expecting to catch the Holy Ghost. As the singing began, I started clapping my hands. I was soon overcome by a wonderful feeling, and before I knew it, I was dancing and jumping all over the place. If memory serves me correctly, I continued jumping and dancing throughout the evangelist's sermon. I repeated this experience for the next couple of nights. I think there was a time of prayer, but I wasn't prayed for. I don't remember the evangelist giving the call for people to come up and get born again. Perhaps he did, but at the conclusion of that revival, I was still without the benefit of salvation. Even so, I had "caught the Holy Ghost." Therefore, I was sure that my life had been changed. At last, I was delivered from the bondage of homosexuality.

Unfortunately, my victory was short-lived. By the end of the week, I nearly succumbed to temptation. By the end of the next week, I had fully succumbed to temptation. Homosexuality was back, and with a vengeance. I remember telling my dad, without going into detail, that the devil was really after me. Oh how I would flee from him in stark terror. But he would catch me every time. The day would eventually come when I would stop, face that demon of homosexuality, and kick it out of my life forever.

But that day was still years away. For the time, I had to deal with the revelation that "catching the Holy Ghost" was not enough to overthrow sin's dominion. It was merely a feel-good experience that in the end had left me terribly disillusioned. And yet, this would begin a perplexing cycle in my life. I would go to church on Sunday and be overcome by those same good feelings. I would dance and jump and really attempt to praise God. At the end of the service, I would leave unsaved and unchanged. Before the next Sunday, I would have already had another homosexual encounter, sometimes more than one. This would happen every time, and it went on for years. The preacher never discussed the plan of salvation. Also, he never gave a call for salvation though he would invariably "open the doors of the church" to solicit membership. Even when I visited with other churches, the outcome was always the same. The devil never bothered me much about going to church. I understand now that was because attending church never threatened, in the least, his control over my life. Please don't misunderstand me. I don't want to leave the impression that there were no churches preaching the gospel. Looking back, I realize that there probably were some. But somehow, I was never able to connect with those churches.

My experiences with churches left me devastated. I mean that if I could not find freedom in the church, then where on earth could it be found? Oh, I continued going to church, because I really enjoyed it. But I was beginning to lose hope that I would be anything other than a homosexual. Perhaps, my friend was right. Perhaps, I needed to accept it. The more I contemplated it, the surer I became that accepting homosexuality was not the right thing to do. But what could I do? Clearly, I could not stop. I was mercilessly at the whim of homosexuality. I knew enough to understand that homosexuality was wrong, but I did not know enough to end its cruel reign in my life: a dark time for me indeed!

Do you know what it's like to feel helpless, trapped with no hope of recovery? Do you know what it's like to hate yourself, to hate your very existence? Do you know what a broken heart feels like? Oh not a heart broken as a result of unrequited romantic love. But a heart crushed by the weight of guilt. If so, then you know how I felt. I ran into so many people who were downright appalled with me. But their disgust was no match for my own. I regularly thought of myself as the scum of the earth. In all honesty, I can tell you that I did not consider anyone more loathsome than myself. It did not matter what kind of vile deed that person had committed.

Add to that the sheer guilt of it all. You see: I wasn't some guy that didn't believe in God. I wasn't mad at the conventional church for telling me homosexuality was a sin. I had read, for myself, the story of the destruction of Sodom and Gomorrah, and frankly it alarmed me. Is this how God felt about me? I wasn't one that was determined to be a homosexual regardless of what the Bible said. I knew God had called me to preach, and I knew that a homosexual preacher is an oxymoron. As a matter of fact, when I was a senior in high school, God used a classmate to drive this point home to me. I shall never forget her. She looked me in the eye and emphatically, without wavering, informed me that an unrepentant homosexual could never be a preacher. I must admit that I argued fiercely with her and left her presence convinced that she was wrong. I took it personally. I loved God, and I knew that I was called to preach the gospel. How could she tell me that I could never be a preacher? However, later when I was alone, her words haunted me. As hard as her words seemed, I knew she was right. In order to fulfill God's plan for my life, I had to give up homosexuality.

And it was revelations like these that would renew in me a will to fight. I thought that I could just make a decision against homosexuality, and it would just go away. I had no idea that I needed power from heaven to back up that decision. It seemed that Satan took great delight in my naiveté and made great sport of me.

Many times, I would go days, weeks and even a few months without a homosexual encounter. During these times, I was sure that I had finally beaten the demon of homosexuality. I would happily announce to my friends that I was no longer a homosexual. I would go about my way happy and excited. I could go to church and praise God with a clear conscience. Praise the Lord—

Hallelujah!—I was free. And then out of nowhere would surface this insuppressible urge to participate in homosexuality again. When it came, I would begin to shake with fear. And then I would grow calm and begin to try to talk myself through to resistance. "Come on, you can do it. You are free, and you can stay free. Don't blow it! Come on, don't do it." But no matter how hard I tried, I was simply no match for the unrelenting urges of my depraved nature. My friends would eventually disbelieve my various proclamations of freedom from homosexuality.

I am sure that the devil laughed at me, as I would rejoice in what I thought was newfound freedom, only to be once again snared in the clutches of homosexuality. This roller coaster of emotions would eventually take its toll on me. Besides, I was perpetually hurt, angry, confused, embittered and scared. I resolved to end my own life. I could think of no other way to end the horror that I was experiencing. Besides, I was so tired of life, and if this was all life had to offer, then why should I go on living? I would come to this point many times where I considered suicide as an option. Each time, however, as I contemplated killing myself, I would be confronted with the words that God had spoken to my heart so long ago: "you will be a husband, a father, and a preacher." And then, I knew that suicide was not my way out. I knew that somehow the words that God spoke to me would someday be fulfilled. If I killed myself, I would never be able to realize my dream of becoming a husband, a father, and a preacher. And suicide was too permanent and irreversible. Therefore, I resolved to simply persevere until freedom came to me. You can see now why I believe that those words literally saved my life.

CHAPTER FIVE

THE TOLL OF HOMOSEXUALITY

In the eleventh chapter of the book of Hebrews, the Bible reveals something about sin that is very important.

> **By faith Moses, when he was come to years, refused to be called the son of Pharaoh's daughter; Choosing rather to suffer affliction with the people of God, than to enjoy the pleasures of sin for a season (Hebrews 11:24,25).**

If you read the Old Testament book of Exodus, you will discover that Moses was a Hebrew child that was reared in the court of Pharaoh. As such, he enjoyed, and was entitled to for the rest of his life, the treasures of Egypt. Discovering the call of God upon his life, he gave up Egypt and all its riches. According to the writer of Hebrews, this action was tantamount to his rejecting the seasonal pleasures of sin. This is merely a capsule version of what Moses had to sacrifice in order to answer the call of God upon his life.

However, what I really want to highlight in this passage of scripture is the fact that sin has pleasure. Homosexuality, adultery, boozing, gambling and drugs all involve a certain amount of gratification. But what most people fail to realize is that the pleasure of sin is only for a season. During the season of pleasure, people are so preoccupied with enjoying themselves that they never think of the consequences of their sins. This is exactly what the devil is counting on. He hopes to get people addicted to the sin during the season of pleasure so that he can later manifest the consequences without much resistance from them. Have you ever wondered why a person would continue smoking cigarettes even after learning that many people have died from smoking? What about the person who has part of his stomach removed because of alcohol-induced bleeding ulcers? The doctor sternly warns him that continued drinking would surely mean death. And yet, he continues to drink. Oh I know we often hear things, such as "if he really wanted to stop drinking, he would." But do you really believe that? I can tell you assuredly that once most people are battered by the penalty of sin, they often crave deliverance. But because the devil has gotten them addicted during the season of pleasure, they are powerless to resist him. And this is why the season of pleasure is so dangerous.

According to Romans 6:23a, "the wages of sin is death." Early in the creation of humanity, God instructed Adam not to eat of the tree of knowledge of good and evil and then informed him of the consequence of disobedience: "for in the day that thou eatest thereof, thou shalt surely die" (Genesis 2:17). When the Bible speaks of death as being a consequence of sin, it is talking about spiritual death, which is separation from God, as opposed to physical death, although spiritual death will eventually produce physical death.

When we are separated from God, we are subject to Satan and all his evil plans against us. When we accept Jesus as our Savior, we destroy the control of Satan over our lives. He never does get to complete his plan against us. However, in the interim—that is, before deliverance comes—the devil succeeds in building up strongholds of hurts in our lives. These hurts, if not dealt with, become mindsets against God, each other and even ourselves. In essence, they make it virtually impossible to attain to a godly and successful life.

This is what I call the toll of sin or, more specifically in my case, the toll of homosexuality. I have included in this chapter a discussion of a few of these attitudes and their negative impact on us. I expect that this discussion will reveal some of these attitudes as being a natural part of your lifestyle. Should that be the case, please take comfort in the fact that I myself have been set free from all the attitudes that I discuss here. Understand also that you too can be delivered.

Fear of God

Immediately after Adam and Eve sinned by disobeying the instructions of God, they did two things that always tell of the entrance of sin. They are both recorded in the third chapter of Genesis. The first in verse 8:

> **And they heard the voice of the Lord God walking in the garden in the cool of the day: and Adam and his wife hid themselves from the presence of the Lord God amongst the trees of the garden.**

The second one is recorded in verses 9 and 10 and gives reason for the first one:

> **And the Lord God called unto Adam, and said unto him, Where art thou? And he said, I heard your voice in the garden, and I was afraid, because I was naked; and I hid myself.**

Adam and Eve introduced sin to this world, and that sin brought with it the fear of God. Now of course, the Bible speaks of a fear of God that is appropriate. But that fear involves a reverence for or an awe of God and inspires obedience. The fear of Genesis 3 involves torment and apprehension. This is the fear that sin inspires.

There are a couple of crucial facts to note about fear and how it changes our attitude against God. First of all, notice that as a result of fear, Adam and Eve hid themselves from God. When God came to visit with Adam on that fateful day, He was simply keeping what had become a wonderful pastime for

Him. He and His family, Adam and Eve, had a perfect relationship. God loved them, and He enjoyed spending time with them. No doubt, Adam and Eve were expecting God. They wanted to be ready for Him when He came. After trying to determine how they would tell God about their latest debacle, they probably just gave up as fear assured them that there was no reasoning with God. When God came to visit His man and woman that day, He discovered that they were no longer eager to spend time with Him. In fact, they had hidden themselves.

To hide yourself from God simply means that you have denied Him access to your life. As a result, He cannot resolve any of the problems in your life. In fact, in your hidden state—without God's help—your only recourse is to become entrenched in your problems. When this happens, we get angry with God because we feel that He has failed us. However, the real problem is that because of sin, we are afraid to go to Him for help. Oh sure, we may utter a few feeble prayers for help. But the bottom line is that sin poisons our attitude against God. It makes us think that God is not really interested in helping us. So even though we may cry out to Him, we are really already convinced that help is not forthcoming.

The second important fact about fear and its impact on our relationship with God is that the dictionary defines *dread*, which is a synonym for *fear*, as *to dislike to experience*. In other words, when we fear God, we dislike experiencing Him. We don't like being around Him. We don't want to have anything to do with Him. Actually if the truth were told, the issue is not so much that we dislike Him but that we believe that He dislikes us. Oh yes, this is what the devil, through our sins, is consistently screaming at us. *God hates you because you are a homosexual, or a drunk, or a thief or a murderer. There is no hope for you because God is against you for your sin.*

Isn't it peculiar how the devil does all he can to drive you to the depths of sin, and then constantly reminds you of God's displeasure for you? He does this to keep you at enmity with God. That way, he can guarantee that you will never receive deliverance from his captivity. Unfortunately, some Christians enforce his diabolical scheme through their own judgmental attitudes.

Now notice that I did not say that you are not guilty. But your guilt does not breed hatred from God. Let me ask you something. If you have a child (or maybe you do), would you automatically hate or disown that child because he stole something, or assaulted another child or used profanity? Then why do you think that God would hate you for your sin? The Bible poses this same question though under different circumstances:

If ye then, being evil, know how to give good gifts unto your children, how much more shall your Father which is in heaven give good things to them that ask him? (Matt. 7:11)

In other words, do you actually think that you're more capable of love than God? Why would God love you any less than you love your children? There really is no reason for you to be confused about how God feels about you. The Bible is clear on this subject. II Corinthians 5:19 tells us that:

God was in Christ, reconciling the world unto Himself, not imputing their trespasses unto them; and has committed unto us the word of reconciliation.

To reconcile is to bring together again in friendship. God has already taken the necessary steps to rekindle friendship with you. If He has reconciled Himself to you, then He cannot still be angry with you.

God's attitude towards you becomes crystal clear when you consider his means of reconciliation. II Corinthians 5:18 says that He did it through Jesus Christ. You are probably able to quote John 3:16 from memory:

For God so loved the world that He gave His only begotten Son, [Jesus Christ] that whosoever believeth in Him should not perish, but have everlasting life.

When God sent Jesus into the world, He released Him to evil men with no regard for righteousness. They beat Jesus beyond recognition. They struck Him repeatedly in the face with their fists. They mocked and cursed Him. They forced Him, bloodied and exhausted, to carry a cross up a hill to a place where they mercilessly crucified Him. Crucifixion was the most inhumane and humiliating form of capital punishment for that day.

When these men came to arrest Jesus to carry Him to His death, He informed them that His Father could send legions of angels to His aid. Later while He suffered horrendously on the cross, His assailants challenged Him to save Himself. If God could help Jesus, why did He leave Him, innocent and without help, to die at the hands of sinful men? Why did not Jesus rise to meet the challenge of His persecutors and deliver Himself from death? John 3:17 answers these questions:

For God sent not His Son into the world to condemn the world, but that the world through Him might be saved.

In other words, God sent His Son to save you from all the evils of this life. Jesus willingly suffered all these things so that you would not be condemned but rather would be brought back into friendship with God. Come now: does this really sound like God is mad with you or that He hates you? Would you yourself do these things for someone you hate? Probably not even for someone you love, but definitely not for someone you hate.

Away with religion! Away with the lies of the devil! I have shown it to you in black and white. Determine now that you will believe the truth that God really does love you and has gone to the max to "make up" with you even though you are the one who has been wrong. What glorious freedom I experienced when I at last understood that God did not hate me for my involvement with homosexuality. That same freedom belongs to you. Do you yet believe God? Why not say aloud the following words:

"Oh God, I am sorry that I have believed the devil's lies for all these years. I see now that you love me, and I love you. And I come to you now asking you to forgive me and set me free from my sins. I accept your offer of friendship through Jesus Christ, and I accept Jesus as my Savior. Amen."

Now walk in the freedom of His love, and refuse to believe again that He hates you. Know also that you can always come to Him, no matter what.

Refusing Blame

Another dangerous mindset caused by sin is the tendency to refuse blame or responsibility for your sin. My wife calls the tendency to pass the blame for your sin the "Adam and Eve Syndrome." You will see why, as you check out how Adam and Eve responded to God when confronted with their sin:

> **"And the man said, the woman whom thou gavest to be with me, she gave me of the tree, and I did eat. And the Lord God said unto the woman, what is this that thou hast done? And the woman said, the serpent beguiled me and I did eat" (Genesis 3:12, 13).**

Immediately, Adam and Eve transferred the blame for their sins to someone else. In fact, Adam blamed both God and Eve—Eve for giving him the fruit, and God for giving him Eve. Now there are at least a couple of reasons that Adam and Eve responded this way. First, they were afraid of the consequences. Perhaps, they thought that they could relax the penalty of death if they could show that someone else was responsible for their sins. Isn't that what we do today? Lawyers hire expert witnesses to show why criminals are not fully responsible for their crimes. And then as a result, jurors reach lesser convictions, and judges hand down lesser sentences.

A second possible reason for the way Adam and Eve responded to God is shame. Adam and Eve's nakedness, which was an absence of the glory of God, was full proof of their sin. They became ashamed. People really do not like to believe that they are as bad as they seem. Theories abound about the innate goodness of mankind. But like Adam and Eve, when we come face to face with our nakedness, we can no longer deny the ugliness of our nature. Shame inevitably sets in. And how do we deal with this shame? We construct an elaborate network of excuses and buck-passing.

I could talk all day about Adam and Eve, but I was really no different. During my struggle with homosexuality, I did my share of buck-passing. I mainly blamed my father for my predicament. I come from a very large family, and while I was growing up, my dad busied himself with trying to provide for us. He spent very little time with me and was hardly ever affectionate. I reasoned that if he had given me the necessary attention as well as assured me of his love, I would never have embraced homosexuality. Eventually, God would convince me that my dad could not be blamed for my problem with homosexuality.

Essentially, this is what homosexuals everywhere have managed to do. When they contend that God created them to be the way they are, then they have effectively passed responsibility for their sin to God. Incidentally, a third reason for buck-passing is to provide justification for the sin. In my own case, if I could just believe that God had created me thus, then I could continue a lifestyle of homosexuality without fear of consequence and without the nagging of a guilty conscience. The problem with that was that I could never find justification for homosexuality in the Bible. Besides that, there was still the matter of that something on the inside that had always been at odds with homosexuality.

If you are involved in homosexuality and have grown weary of its toll, then you are going to have to be honest about some things. Admit that homosexuality is a sin. Admit also that you and you alone are responsible for your struggle with homosexuality. This is the case even if you were molested as a young boy. You might be interested in knowing that it was only after I assumed responsibility for homosexuality that I was able to destroy its hold over my life. It will be no different for you.

Insecurity

There are many other detrimental mindsets, which result from homosexuality, but insecurity will be the last one that we shall discuss. This is partly because insecurity encapsulates so many of the other mindsets. And also I believe that by the end of this discussion, I would have armed you with enough information to bring you lasting freedom from these mindsets.

Sin absolutely breeds insecurity, especially if it is an addictive and controlling sin like homosexuality. And especially when you grow tired of the sin but realize that you are powerless to stop it. When a person is insecure, he is uncertain not only about himself but how he relates to God and the world around him. He fluctuates uncontrollably. He may feel good about himself today, and tomorrow may be nearly suicidal. He fluctuates also concerning God and other people. Insecurity is especially dangerous because it is a breeding ground for a nest of deadly emotions.

Zest for Approval

A person who is struggling with insecurity very much needs other people to validate his importance. And herein lies also his need for approval. An insecure person often goes overboard in pursuing the attention and affection of others. He absolutely cannot exist without it. He is the person who would spend hours agonizing over a comment made by someone else perhaps in jest or without serious intent. He takes all criticism, no matter how positive or constructive, directly to heart. He is a crowd pleaser and often does things strictly for the approval of others. I remember in high school that I was exactly this way. I would do homework for other students, shower them with gifts and flatter them excessively, all to get them to like me. A person like this could never fully surrender to God because he is too concerned about what others think of him.

Contempt

Contempt doesn't readily seem to be an attribute of a person who is dedicated to winning the approval of others. What happens though is that a person eventually grows tired of being so controlled by others and their opinions. He resents always feeling that he is inferior to them. So then ultimately, his insecurity moves from the stage of seeking approval to expressing contempt. I experienced this. Years later, the people from whom I had desperately sought approval had suddenly become the object of my disgust.

Deceit

A person could hardly win and keep the approval of others without the employment of deceit. I was no exception. I learned very early to deceive people, making them believe what I wanted them to believe. Rarely would I express disagreement with them for fear of losing their approval. I was the quintessential diplomat, hardly ever provoking my peers to emotional outbursts. I did not say what I believed; I said what they wanted to hear. By college, I certainly knew how to use deceit to my advantage. I could feign hurt to draw affectionate hugs of sympathy. I could pretend offense that would cause people to beg my forgiveness. And I could pretend happiness when I was all broken up inside.

Distrust

One reason that an insecure person is so deceitful is because he is as unsure of other people as he is of himself. For all his efforts to gain the approval of other people, he essentially distrusts them. Because he is so consumed with self-hatred, he is convinced that other people hate him as well, or they would certainly hate him if only they knew the real him. And so he uses deceit as a means of constructing walls of protection in his life. For fear of being rejected, he is leery of letting people get too close to him. And so the walls are his way of maintaining a safe distance between him and other people.

I can tell you that as a person that struggled with homosexuality for a number of years, I was subjected to all these emotions and many more. I did not make them up, or hear about them in some psychology class. I experienced them. For a painfully long time, I was an emotional quagmire. My negative mindsets would begin to affect every part of my life. I was crippled in having even simple friendships with other people. Moreover, my lack of authenticity only resulted in greater bouts of self-delusion. Even my grades in college plummeted. I was an emotional wreck going somewhere to happen.

But I can also tell you that today I stand free of all of these emotions. None of them threaten my happiness or sanity. I no longer lie awake at night ravaged by guilt and shame. I no longer seek the approval of others. I am free; and I didn't have to spend heartrending hours on some psychiatrist's couch in order to obtain my freedom. Jesus set me free through His blood and His love that I have so endeavored to express in this book. Perhaps, you can relate to the emotions I've expressed in this chapter. Perhaps, this section has evoked some painful emotions for you. Maybe now, you are even crying, just wanting the pain to be over forever. I want you to know that the same Jesus that set me free is waiting so eagerly to do the same for you. Take comfort, my friend, as I remind you of some of the vital points of this chapter:

God is no longer angry with you but has taken great measure to bring you into friendship with Himself.

You must resolve never to deny God access to your life, but rather come to Him even when you are wrong.

Take responsibility for your sin regardless of what it is and accept the freedom that God offers (AND)

Know that not only does God offer you deliverance from homosexuality (or any sin) but He also wants to free you forever from the emotional toll of homosexuality.

Chapter Six

FREE AT LAST

As I have said, sin does have pleasure but the pleasure of sin is not worth the exacted cost. Homosexuality was fast taking its toll on my life. By the time I graduated from high school, I was a mere shell of a person. What should have been one of the happiest times of my life turned out to be marked by misery, and regret for having spent so many years of my life cheated by homosexuality. I wistfully wondered what it would have been like if I had lived as my peers, essentially free of homosexuality. I mourned the fact that I would never know. What troubled me greatly was that I was now entering adulthood with the same baggage that I woefully carried around during adolescence. I was beginning to think that homosexuality was indeed my destined and inescapable plight.

What's more, the words that I had heard in my heart as a young boy, that had so buoyed me many times during my struggle, were growing increasingly dim. Would I ever really know what it would be like to be a husband, a father and a preacher?

But as far as I could tell, there was a silver lining, dull though it was, behind my dark cloud. I was scheduled to go off to college after the summer. For a number of reasons, I was excited about leaving home and attending college. Ever desperate for hope, however, I imagined that perhaps going off to college would prove to be my big break—that is, my break from homosexuality. I thought that if I could just get away from my old life, my old influences and my old environment, then maybe I would have a chance of forging a new life free of homosexuality.

That summer could not pass fast enough, but finally it did. I arrived at Young Harris College in Your Harris, Georgia early in the fall of 1982. Young Harris College is nestled against a backdrop of the Georgia Mountains, which provide a scenic view all year long. Surrounded by such beautiful scenery, I was tempted to forget all the troubles I had left at home. As I began to make new friends and new and better memories, I was sure that homosexuality would soon become resigned to my past. Oh for sure, I still had the feelings. But somehow—I still am not sure just how—I managed to refrain from homosexual activities while at college. I felt so safe, so destined for a better life. Homosexuality seemed as far away from me as the hundreds of miles that separated my hometown from my present domicile.

Imagine then my chagrin when while at home during a break from college, I succumbed once again to homosexuality. And this happened every time I was home from college. I just could not believe it! How on earth could I go for months, while at college, without the slightest incidence of homosexuality? And then at home, I would find myself helplessly overcome by temptation. I just couldn't figure it out. I finally concluded rather naively that homosexuality, at least for me, was a demon whose main hangout was my hometown. Even so, each experience with homosexuality brought back the misery of my past and cast a shadow over my happiness at Young Harris College.

In the summer of 1984, I was home working and preparing to enroll that fall at Oglethorpe University in Atlanta. I had been accepted at Oglethorpe after graduating with an Associate's Degree from Young Harris College. At home, I was re-living my continuing saga with homosexuality. I found myself again unable to deny the demands of my feelings. Clearly, homosexuality was in control. And clearly, homosexuality had taken its toll. I was more depressed, more despondent and more disillusioned than I had ever been. And I had completely given up on ever fulfilling my childhood dreams. Even if I did manage somehow to break free from homosexuality, what woman would agree to be my wife after being confronted by my past?

Towards the end of the summer, I left my hometown determined never to return. I just could not stand to live there another day. For me, it had simply become a place of great anguish—a place of consistent failure. There, I had failed to resist feelings of homosexuality. There, after being overwhelmed by temptation, I had failed to break the vicious cycle of homosexuality in my life. There, I had failed to develop a relationship with God. There, I had failed to gain the respect of my peers. And I was tired of failing, tired of hope deferred and tired of nurturing a heart broken—no, dashed to pieces—by the cruel, relentless blows of homosexuality.

And so I bought a ticket and boarded a greyhound headed for Atlanta and a new school year. As the bus carried me miles away from my pain, I could not help but wonder: "Could this be a new beginning for me; would I at last find freedom from homosexuality?" *There it goes again*, I thought, *that small, insuppressible glimmer of hope*. For all these years, it had been as tenacious as homosexuality itself. But to what avail? Was I still not caught helplessly in the death grip of homosexuality? I pushed it out of my mind. I was through with relying on false hopes.

I arrived in Atlanta a few weeks before the start of the fall semester. So I accepted the offer to board with the family of one of my college friends. His family actually was as much my friends as he was. His parents accepted me into their home and treated me as one of their own children. They included me in all their family activities and proudly introduced me to their friends. They even listened, with sympathetic ears, as I shared with them some of the pain I had experienced in my young life. Of course, I was too ashamed to tell them everything. I'm sure that by now, you can guess what part I left out.

I especially remember one particularly endearing thing they did for me. The parents offered to take me to Oglethorpe to begin the fall semester.

Although I was a junior, it was my first year at Oglethorpe, and so I had to endure all the formalities that freshmen endure. I fully expected them to drop me off with a few fond farewells. Instead, they spent most of the day with me. They helped get me registered and moved into the dorm. Before they finally left, they ensured that I had everything I needed to have a successful semester at school. No one had ever done this for me. Their love and selfless generosity truly affected me. In fact, that family had such a positive impact on me that it has lasted even unto this day.

At any rate, while I was spending the remaining weeks of the summer at their home, I became more keenly aware of my desperate longing for God. It seemed that my thinking became clearer in that quiet and peaceful environment. Whatever the case, I knew that things could not continue as they were. In fact, it seemed that I could sense that change was on the horizon. Yet, I had no idea how such change could ever take place. I was simply too battered by the trials of my life to cause such change to be. If it were to be, it had to come from somewhere beyond myself. I was too weak to continue the fight.

Alas, homosexuality had made its final conquest. It had managed to vanquish every ounce of resolve from my battered spirit. Every part of me seemed to say: "Okay, I give up; you win." I felt that my heart would literally break apart. All I wanted to do was close my eyes and pass peacefully into oblivion.

The time to begin school at Oglethorpe University finally arrived. As I once again settled in to the experience of college living, I could not help but think of how unhappy I had become. Sure, I was attending a great school. And yes, many friends and fond memories enriched my life. There was also a little family in Stone Mountain, Georgia that had succeeded in making me feel really important. But the thing I wanted most, after all these years, still proved to be the most elusive.

I joined the college's chapter of the Baptist Student Union merely out of religious habit. While attending one of the Bible studies one evening, I looked around the room, noticing the expression of joy on the faces of many in attendance. Could it be that these people were genuinely happy? Better yet, could they connect me to the joy I saw on their faces? I wouldn't find out that evening because I would not open up to anyone. I reasoned within myself that if I opened up to them, I was sure what the outcome would be. And I just was not willing to endure rejection at this point in my life. Besides, how could I really know if they were genuinely happy? Even I, in times of gross unhappiness, had managed to fake those same smiles I saw plastered on their faces. In fact, at that very meeting, I was feigning happiness. However, mere pretense had gotten the better of me. I had really grown tired of pretending and was longing everyday for something real. Little did I know how close I was to finally getting what I had always wanted.

There is a wonderful passage of scripture that I absolutely must share with you at this point:

> **"How beautiful upon the mountains are the feet of him that bringeth good tidings, that publisheth peace; that bringeth good tidings of good, that publisheth salvation; that saith unto Zion, Thy God reigneth!" (Isaiah 52:7)**

As I read this scripture now, I am reminded of the Emancipation Proclamation. The Emancipation Proclamation was great news for African American slaves who had fought untiringly against the atrocity of slavery. We normally think of Abraham Lincoln as being the originator of such glad tidings. But how sweet must have been the voice that broke the news over the airwaves that day. And how precious must have been the sight of the jubilant slave, running from plantation to plantation to share the news with fellow slaves. In essence, people who bring good news are welcomed sights to those who have long awaited such news.

My good-news bearer was a gentleman by the name of Kyle Holland. And just like those slaves, I would be greeted with news of liberty, but liberty of a different kind. I would learn that Jesus had died to bring peace into my life and to save me from the dominion of sin. His death and subsequent resurrection had made it possible for the God of Heaven to live and reign in my life.

Kyle was the assistant pastor of a local Atlanta church that was committed to bringing the gospel of Christ to college students. Members of the church would visit college campuses throughout the city, share the gospel with students, and try to encourage them to give their lives to Christ. That day, I would be the student that Kyle encountered. The one thing that I remember about Kyle to this day is that his eyes seemed to be filled with compassion and love. Indeed, it seemed that as I looked into his face, I was staring into the eyes of Jesus. I had never before (nor yet since) seen such eyes of love.

Kyle began our conversation by opening up a small booklet. He said that his church was conducting a survey among college students and that he was soliciting my participation. I must confess I had no idea that this was an evangelistic tactic. Even when he read the so-called survey question, I still did not catch on. The question: ***Do you believe you are going to heaven when you die and why or why not?*** The survey then listed a number of reasons you could choose from to support your answer. I answered in the affirmative though rather reluctantly. But when I perused the list of reasons, I immediately saw two that grabbed my attention. Surely, they were the right answers.

My first choice: *because I believe in God*. I must say that I was quite confident. That was a no-brainer! Surely, everybody knew that if you believe in God, you get to go to heaven when you die. But Kyle wasted no time in revealing to me that belief in God alone did not automatically qualify a person for heaven. In fact, he showed me a scripture that expressed those sentiments exactly:

> **"Thou believest that there is one God; thou doest well: the devils also believe, and tremble" (James 2:19).**

I was amazed to see, from the Bible, that my belief alone in one God was nothing more than mere concession to a universal fact. Whoop de doo! Even the devil believed this.

A little sheepish, I quickly voiced my second choice: *I am a good person*. Yes, this had to be the right answer. Of course, that first answer was wrong. I mean, there are so many people that believe in one God, and yet they are not good people. I thought about my own self. Sure, I was a homosexual. But at heart, I was a good person. I didn't smoke, drink or use profanity. I was very kind and generous to people. I loved everyone genuinely, or so I thought. I was obedient to my parents, and I was at college trying to make something out of my life. So yes, I thought, that's got to be the answer. *I believe in God, and I am a good person.*

It is amazing that a person, so riddled by guilt and shame as I was, can, when the occasion warrants, summon the esteem to commend himself. I was exhibiting one of those dangerous mindsets I spoke of in chapter five: the refusal to admit that I was sinful. I just could not let my guard down. What I did not realize was that the guard that I so adamantly kept up was effective in keeping out the help that I so desperately needed. Fortunately, for me, Kyle would do all he could to break down my guard.

As I mouthed my second choice, I looked incredulously at Kyle as he declined my answer with a casual shake of his head. It was hard to be frustrated with him though he kept insisting that I was wrong about God and heaven. Something about him drew me, in spite of myself. There was a wonderful expression of joy on his face. It was as though he was on the verge of revealing to me a marvelous secret, one that would change my life forever. It was my turn to listen intently as Kyle began to share with me the good news of liberty in Christ Jesus.

He explained to me why being good was not the way into heaven. God is perfect, and the fact of the matter is that we could never within ourselves be good enough to obtain God's approval. When Adam and Eve sinned, they opened the door for sin to enter and corrupt the entire human race. As a result, man even at his best will always find himself far below God's standard of righteousness. Therefore, he could never, depending on his own efforts at all, enter into the kingdom of heaven. So man desperately needed a mediator, someone who could stand on his behalf and in his place, paying the penalty for sin and making man once again acceptable to God.

> **"For there is one God, and one MEDIATOR between God and men, the man CHRIST JESUS; who gave himself a ransom for all, to be testified in due time" (I Tim. 2:5, 6).**

The mediator was none other than Jesus Christ, the Righteous. He willingly paid for the sins of humanity with his own righteous blood. Jesus is like a bridge between humanity and God. By accepting the work that Jesus has already accomplished on man's behalf, a person can walk across that bridge right into the waiting arms of God. The only other alternative is to approach God with your own good works. And frankly, no work of man, no matter how good, could ever measure up to God's expectations.

Is this really a surprise, though? How often do we ourselves lament the imperfection of our humanness? We long to be thinner or taller. We make resolutions to swear less, to quit smoking and to treat people better. We consistently scold ourselves for the decisions we make. Let's face it: we are often out of favor with ourselves. Dare we think it strange that God has standards that we cannot meet? The good news is that God has provided a way—and only one way—for us to come permanently into His favor. Jesus is that way. In writing to the Galatians, Paul was explicit on this very point:

> **Knowing that a man is not justified by the works of the law (or his own good works), but by the faith of Jesus Christ, even we have believed in Jesus Christ, that we might be justified by the faith of Christ, and not by the works of the law: for by the works of the law (or a man's good works) shall no flesh (or no one) be justified (Galatians 2:16, parentheses mine).**

I sat riveted as Kyle continued to share the gospel with me. I had been in church all my life, but I had never heard anything like this. Could it be that God—oh no, perish the thought, too good the thought—that God had actually made a way out of homosexuality? The question burned in my heart. As I looked into Kyle's eyes, my body began to relax a little, and I began to drop my guard. Somehow, I knew that I could trust him. My mouth somehow found the courage to utter a confession that had rarely escaped my lips: "I am a homosexual." My heart seemed to be pleading: "Is there also hope for me?" Kyle must have read my heart's plea in my eyes because he began to immediately assure me that God's love and forgiveness was for homosexuals too.

The revelation was almost too wonderful to contemplate. The God of the entire universe loves me? Insignificant, abominable me? Me, the homosexual? Me: feminine mannerisms and all? Me, the lost cause? Peaceless, restless, faithless me? Though intrigued, I was completely taken aback by Kyle's next question: "Would you like to accept Jesus into your life?"

I was even less prepared for the internal battle that ensued. What was so hard about this? Surely, I wanted to be free of homosexuality. I quietly worried about the consequences. Could I give up my friends and my personal interests? Was I really ready for such a total lifestyle change? Kyle had not mentioned any of these things to me, but somehow I knew that God was interested only in a serious commitment from me. With doubt and indecision raging in my heart, I managed to answer yes to Kyle's question. But there was no fooling Kyle. He simply looked at me with kind resolve and said, "No, you are not ready." And then he walked away.

At the time, I completely misunderstood Kyle's response to my expressed desire to accept Christ into my life. After all, I had answered yes to his question. Why was he insisting that I was not ready? In retrospect, however, I realize that Kyle was not interested in just obtaining another star for his soul-winning crown. I was not some conquest to him. He knew better than most Christians do today that a conversion experience has a more lasting impact for the person that genuinely desires to be converted. Noticing the doubt and confusion in my eyes, he knew that it would be wise to wait until I could come to Jesus in faith. Over the years, I have grown to greatly appreciate his discretion.

However, for the rest of that day and the next, I was consumed with memories of my conversation with Kyle. For the life of me, I could not figure out why I was so reluctant. This seemed like the very thing I had been praying for all my life. Why was I so afraid? What was holding me back? Later, I ran into Kyle on one of the patios of the college. I was eager to talk with him, so we found some place quiet to talk. He shared the same message with me about Christ, which was just as compelling as before. He repeated the same question. I gave the same answer with the same reservations in my heart. Again Kyle said, "No, you are not ready."

I left the patio that day a little confused but still with the message of Jesus burning in my heart. I simply could not shake it from my mind. It was beginning to consume me. Later while in my room waiting for an afternoon meeting with the Baptist Student Union, I fell asleep. While asleep, I was overcome by a strange sensation. It seemed to me then, and even now, to be just a part of a dream. However, when I awakened and went to the meeting, a fellow student greeted me, inquiring about my well-being. I remember distinctly saying to her, "I feel strange; I feel as though I have just undergone surgery." Hearing myself say those words was even stranger. I did not know what they meant. I only knew how I felt. Little did I know I was one of the fishes of which Jesus spoke in the book of Matthew chapter 4, verses 18 and 19. And he was gradually reeling me in.

That evening, I attended a mini gospel concert to which Kyle had invited me. It was held on campus. I thoroughly enjoyed the concert, as it featured both singing and preaching of the gospel. I was just as spellbound as when Kyle had presented the gospel to me on those two occasions. I still, however, failed to respond to the altar call. Immediately after the concert, four young men cornered me. I listened intently as they excitedly shared the gospel with me. Kyle came over and "rescued" me, concerned that I might be overwhelmed.

Finally, the concert was over. Lights were out, and people began filing out of the building and to their cars. I began walking back to my dorm, a walk that seemed so much longer than the two hours before when I had eagerly taken it to the concert. My heart was heavy, as I grappled with the decision that every person must inevitably face. I just could not understand why it was so hard. Back in my room, I was relieved to find that my roommate was still out for the evening. As I lay on my bed, my mind fraught with confusion, I clearly heard the voice of God, "Why are you hesitating? This is what you've wanted all your life. Don't be afraid. Go for it"

What I've wanted all my life? *My heart's desire*? Where had I heard those words before? It was coming back to me now, slowly at first, and then clearly and steadily. I was a teenage worker at the local sawmill in my hometown. I was engrossed in my work, so I did not see him when he approached me. He was a young boy, not much older than myself. I didn't remember his name—didn't remember if he had even identified himself. He had simply informed me that he had a word from God for me. He said that God had sent him to let me know that He loved me, and that He was going to give me my heart's desire.

It seems strange to me now, but at the time, I accepted him as being a genuine oracle of God. In fact, I was rather fond of the idea that God desired to communicate with me. My heart palpitated with restrained excitement as I contemplated his words: *God wanted to give me my heart's desire. How wonderful—oh my, really, my heart's desire. Thank you, Lord*!

There was just one problem however; for the life of me, I could not figure out what my heart desire was. I conducted an intense search of my heart, and could only come up with two really pressing desires. I wanted to graduate from high school with honors, and I wanted to go to college. But those hardly seemed like heart desires—strong desires, perhaps, but not the very longing of my soul. Nevertheless, those desires were granted; so eventually, I took them to be the ones God had meant.

But then, as I lay on my bed, I was hearing those same words: "Don't be afraid, this is what you've always wanted. This is your heart's desire!" That was it! That was what I needed! As those words reverberated through my very being, I was instantly set free from indecision. I raced down the sidewalk to the Student Center where the concert had been held, praying that Kyle was still around. This time, I would not be denied. As I rushed through the double doors into the building, I was relieved to see that Kyle was talking on one of the pay phones. Thank God, I was not too late! When Kyle concluded his telephone conversation, I informed him that I was ready to become a Christian.

This time, Kyle did not question my sincerity. He did, however, invite me out for a late night snack. We went down the street to Waffle House. Fond as I was of hamburger and hash browns, I must confess that the meal was not the highlight of my visit to Waffle House that evening. It was there at Waffle House that Kyle shared more of the gospel with me. And best of all, it was there that God dealt the mortal blow to homosexuality. I was free at last.

Chapter Seven

OH NO! NOT AGAIN!

I was born again. I was a brand new person, and God had forgiven all my sins, including homosexuality. I was so happy, so grateful to be finally free. But the good news was not over yet. Kyle asked me if I wanted to receive the baptism of the Holy Spirit. *The baptism of the Holy Spirit? What is that?* I had heard of "catching the Holy Ghost," but this baptism thing was completely foreign to me. Kyle mentioned something about speaking in tongues, but I thought it was for really good people—you know, folks who really had it going on with God. Surely, someone like me could never speak in tongues. On the other hand, just a few hours ago, I had been hesitant about giving my heart to Jesus. And yet, it turned out to be just what I needed. Perhaps, this tongues thing should not be taken lightly. I told Kyle that I was interested.

We left Waffle House and traveled to an apartment where some other men lived. They were all members of Kyle's church. I recognized them as being the four guys that had so eagerly witnessed to me at the concert. After the proper introductions, Kyle immediately opened the Bible and began to explain to me about the baptism in the Holy Spirit with the evidence of speaking in tongues.

> **And when the day of Pentecost was fully come, they were all with one accord in one place. And suddenly there came a sound from heaven as a rushing mighty wind, and it filled all the house where they were sitting. And there appeared unto them cloven tongues like as of fire, and it sat upon each of them. And they were all filled with Holy Ghost, and began to speak with other tongues, as the Spirit gave them utterance (Acts 2:1-4).**

Kyle began to explain to me that it was God's will for me to receive the Holy Spirit. He also explained that when he put his hands on me and prayed, I would suddenly have the urge to say something. I was to speak it, and when it came out, it would be tongues. This may sound a little incredible to you, but I bought it hook, line and sinker. Kyle had helped me so tremendously when he led me to the Lord that I was willing to believe anything he had to say.

And because of this basic faith in the words that I was hearing, I instantly received the Holy Spirit while Kyle was still talking. With considerable difficulty, however, I held back the tongues, waiting for the moment when Kyle would place his hands on me. For I thought that the laying on of hands was prerequisite to my speaking in tongues. When Kyle finally prayed, I seemed to burst forth in tongues, much like water long held at bay by a dam that has finally been demolished.

Words, however elegant, could never adequately express the joy that coursed through my soul. At last, God had broken through my self-constructed walls and rescued me from the devil's camp to life in His kingdom, at peace and blessedly forgiven of my sins.

> **"Who [God] hath delivered us from the power of darkness, and hath translated us into the kingdom of His dear Son: In whom we have redemption through his blood, even the forgiveness of sins" (Colossians 1:13, 14).**

As my life began to change, one of the first things I noticed was that I was no longer desperately seeking the approval of other people. I even marveled that I could eat lunch or dinner at school without requiring the company of my friends. And I certainly enjoyed my new friends: Kyle and all the members of his church. But what I appreciated most of all was that I was no longer having to fight feelings of homosexuality. I was free.

Gradually, I was beginning to hear and understand the voice of God when He spoke to me. Once, I was at a men's meeting that was sponsored by my church. My pastor and Kyle were teaching the men how to conduct themselves as husbands and fathers. I quickly concluded that the meeting did not apply to me. I had long decided that like Paul, I would remain unmarried and simply live in service to the Lord. You understand of course that I was being driven more by my past than a genuine desire to be single.

The pastor ended the meeting by praying for each man. As he prayed for me, I sensed the Holy Spirit saying to my heart, "You are no Paul." I knew instantly exactly what He meant. And then He reminded me of the words I had heard as a little boy: "You will be a husband, a father and a preacher." And for the first time in my life, I realized that God Himself had authored those words. I knew then, for sure, that one day despite my past, I would be happily married.

That semester was the happiest of my life as I discovered more and more of the goodness of God. But it would soon be time for me to visit my family for the Christmas holidays. At home, I was still excited by my newfound relationship with God. The holidays passed slowly as I waited impatiently to return to school and my new friends. However, when it was time to return, I would be stopped dead in my tracks by what I thought was God's instructions to stay at home. I was chagrined! Didn't God know that school was the most important thing to me? What possible good reason could there be for asking me to give up school? I believed that God would allow me to return to school again one day, but this did not make it any easier to obey Him.

In retrospect, it seems silly, but at the time, I completely misinterpreted God's instructions. Years later, I realized that God deals with people on an individual basis, and as an individual, I personally required high spiritual maintenance. There were some areas in my life that posed a threat to the fulfillment of God's plan for my life. As such, they demanded serious and uninterrupted attention. The bottom line: school could wait! If only I had been spiritually astute then, I would have more fully cooperated with God. And I would have saved myself considerable hardship and grief.

At any rate, I did not return to Oglethorpe University and Atlanta. At home, I was able to connect with a family that was really serious about the things of God. Through them, I learned so much about God and felt myself growing stronger spiritually with each passing day. Sometimes, we would spend hours just talking about God and His goodness. Those were difficult times because I so desperately missed college. However, because of my relationship with that family, they were some of the most exciting times of my life.

After about a year and a half, I left Georgia and went to Tampa, Florida to spend some time with one of my older sisters. From there, I moved to Orlando, Florida. It was in Orlando that the tide would begin to change in a way that took me completely by surprise. All the time I was basking in the goodness of God, I had lost sight of one of the devil's most deadly characteristics: perseverance.

> **"Be sober, be vigilant because your adversary the devil, as a roaring lion, walketh about, seeking whom he may devour" (1Peter 5:8).**

I had relaxed my vigil because I thought that I would not be bothered with the demon of homosexuality again. Little did I realize that he was on the outskirts, looking and waiting for an entrance back into my life.

All my life while involved in homosexuality, I had lived under the strong arm of condemnation. I had strongly disapproved of myself, as I was sure that God and others had. When I got saved, homosexuality left instantly, but condemnation lingered. At the time, I was not aware that there was something that I could do about condemnation.

> "There is therefore now no condemnation to them, which are in Christ Jesus, who walk not after the flesh, but after the Spirit. For the law of the Spirit of life in Christ Jesus hath made me free from the law of sin and death" (Romans 8:1, 2).

When Paul wrote this, he was writing to Christians. The Bible had already declared that I had been set free from condemnation. This meant that I didn't have to be condemned by anything from my past, or my present, for that matter. I only needed to believe this and say it every time the devil came to me with feelings of condemnation. But I held my peace when the devil came on the scene with his insinuations about God not really having forgiven me. Let me assure you that when the devil is speaking to you, the absolute worst thing you can do is to hold your peace.

Because of condemnation, I had a very difficult time forgetting and forgiving my past. I knew that I was a Christian, but I often ashamedly wondered how I had allowed myself to become so involved in homosexuality. People usually do judge the book by its cover. So because I still had very strong feminine mannerisms, people, including Christians, failed to understand that I had been set free from homosexuality. And some of them still wanted nothing to do with me.

Consequently, some of my old mindsets began to re-surface. When Christians especially doubted my deliverance, I was left hurt and bewildered. And ultimately, I began to seek the approval of others again. The irony was that the person whose approval alone I needed had already granted it and had set me free from condemnation. Unfortunately, I overlooked this one significant fact and began to entertain thoughts of inadequacy. Despite my new life in Christ, I began to really feel that I did not measure up. This is exactly what the devil wanted. Because when I succumbed to my feelings of inadequacy, I was in effect depending on myself instead of Christ for my justification with God. I was doing exactly what Paul had scolded the Galatians for doing:

> "Are ye so foolish? Having begun in the Spirit, are you now made perfect by the flesh?" (Galatians 3:3)

In other words, I had begun this life of freedom through complete trust in Jesus and His righteousness. Now, I was trying in vain to continue it through my own self-worth. Paul was concerned about the inevitable outcome of such behavior:

> **"But now, after that ye have known God, or rather are known of God, how turn ye again to the weak and beggarly elements, whereunto ye desire again to be in BONDAGE?" (Galatians 4:9)**

The operative word here is *bondage*. There is no power in the flesh to deliver and certainly not to maintain deliverance. Therefore, a person who places confidence in the flesh, or himself, is doomed to repeat the bondage from which he was delivered. So unbeknownst to me, I was courting a re-visitation of homosexuality. And all this was because of condemnation, something from which I had already gained freedom. I just did not know it.

But I was doing something else that virtually guaranteed the devil a place in my life. I had stopped going to church, or even home Bible studies, for that matter. Of course, I know now that this was in direct violation of the Word of God:

> **"And let us consider one another to provoke unto love and to good works: Not forsaking the assembling of ourselves together, as the manner of some is; but exhorting one another: and so much the more, as ye see the day approaching" (Hebrews 10:24, 25).**

When we abandon fellowship with other Christians, we put ourselves in a precarious position where the devil is concerned. Of course, one Christian armed with the power of God can, by himself and on a bad day, totally annihilate the devil's plans. So the concern is not one of weakness but one of deception. Eve was not weak; she was deceived. The devil didn't dare challenge Adam and Eve's authority until he had successfully robbed them of the Word of God. His techniques are still the same. His angle is to steal the Word of God from your heart—the word that you are saved. The word that you are important to Christ, and with Him, you are all that you need to be. The word that there is no condemnation to people who are in Christ Jesus. When he has successfully stolen the word from your heart, he can and will challenge with ease your authority to be who you are. To be saved. To be free from homosexuality. To go to heaven when you die. When this happens, you are at the very door of your old lifestyle.

God is not ignorant of the devil's devices—and we should not be!—and has designed a system that will thwart his schemes every time. That system involves the church. That system is fellowshipping with the saints. So many times throughout the years, I have been encouraged by other people to maintain my stand for Christ even in the midst of difficult situations. I am a pastor now and at times am encouraged by my own preaching. But even before my pastorate, rarely did I leave my church, after having heard my pastor preach, without the urge to live better for Christ, to be more cooperative with God. To consecrate my life more wholly to God. The Bible calls this *provoking one another to love and good works*. And it is accomplished in the context of the assembly of Christians.

In this scripture, the Bible also speaks of "exhorting one another." To exhort means *to urge strongly, advise or warn earnestly*. How many times have I entered a church, depressed, discouraged, and just tired of the fight, and left invigorated and determined to surmount all of the devil's obstacles? I was able to do this only after encountering the exhortation of the saints: their strong urging and advice to persevere in the things of God. And how many times have I decided to walk circumspectly before God after being earnestly warned by some preacher about the perils of sin?

Besides that, there are a number of benefits that can be found in the congregation of the righteous. There is information, revelation, enlightenment and inspiration. There are prayer lines that can generate healing, strength for adversity and salvation for loved ones. And the manifestation of the presence of the Holy Spirit is absolutely contagious. When I see people genuinely dance, sing and laugh under the inspiration of the Holy Spirit, I am encouraged to add my own praises to God. I am so grateful that God is so good to so many people.

But I didn't know then what I know now. I foolishly stopped going to church when there was a number of good churches in my area. As I did this, condemnation gradually returned to my life and grew to the point where it overwhelmed me. I know for a fact that had I been involved in a good church, I never would have accepted the devil's condemnation. But I did, and as a result, I was soon in his grip again. Oh yes, you've guessed it by now: I became involved with homosexuality again. I was incredulous. How had this happened? All I could think was *Oh no! Not again! Not again*!

There really is no need for me to prolong this chapter by discussing all the emotions I experienced as a consequence of my second bout with homosexuality. Suffice it to know, that things were even worse than before. I will, however, as a postscript to this chapter, inform you that you don't have to suffer what I went through. If you have received deliverance from any type of bondage, determine that you will regularly fellowship with Christians. Become a part of a really good church and attend faithfully. Find some good teaching/preaching via media and embrace it. Whatever you do, do not alone face the wiles of the devil. I stiffen with incredulity when I recall the words of one well-meaning Christian, who suggested that God sent me back into homosexuality to prove that He could deliver me. Nothing is further from the truth. Nothing is more asinine. What happened to me was absolutely unnecessary. It was never God's will for me to become entangled again by the yokes of homosexuality. He wasn't trying to teach me something. He wasn't trying to keep me humble. I did this to myself.

Nevertheless, here was I: a homosexual for the second time around! Born-again and tongues talking! What was a guy to do? How would I ever make it through?

Chapter Eight

INVINCIBLE LOVE
PART ONE

As I once again waded through the murky waters of homosexuality, I often found myself aloof and deeply contemplative. I simply could not believe that I was practicing homosexuality again. Of course, I tried denial at first. Perhaps, this was just a momentary relapse that would not repeat itself. But as the days passed and the encounters became more frequent, I had to finally admit that homosexuality was again a sad reality in my life.

But now, I was somewhat confused—okay, I was totally confused. I mean, here I was a born-again, tongues-talking believer. I knew for certain that I had encountered God and that my life had been wonderfully impacted by that encounter. I could still remember the joy of His presence. And yet, I had been overtaken by sin. It just did not seem possible. What on earth had gone wrong?

Of course, in retrospect, my confusion seems ludicrous. I could sit down today and, without much thought, explore with any backslider the reasons for his backsliding. But I had little knowledge then of what I've shared with you in the previous chapter. So as it were, I was as dumbfounded and consequently subdued as a conquering hero by a sudden and deadly strike from a vanquished and long forgotten enemy.

Confusion, however, was not chief among my concerns. I worried about God's love for me now that I had returned to homosexuality. I felt as Adam and Eve must have felt in the wake of their treason against God. I had it all—joy, peace, victory, and freedom—and in one swift moment of weakness, I had surrendered it all to the enemy of my soul.

Genesis 27 tells a powerful story of how one man was tricked out of the blessing of his birthright. When Isaac would have proclaimed blessings of prosperity and dominion over Esau, Jacob, coached by his mother, disguised himself as Esau and thereby received the blessings that were meant for Esau. Of course, Jacob was far from innocent in his dealings with Esau, but to prevent an unwarranted exoneration of Esau, we would do well to consider a particular passage of scripture:

> **And Esau said to Jacob, Feed me, I pray thee, with that same red pottage...And Jacob said, Sell me this day thy birthright. And Esau said, Behold, I am at the point to die...what profit shall this birthright do to me? And he sold his birthright unto Jacob...thus Esau despised his birthright (Genesis 25:30-34).**

Esau was merely hungry, not at all at the point of death as he claimed. But instead of summoning one of the many household servants to bring him food, he sold his birthright for a pot of stew. And so when the day came for Isaac to hand out blessings, Jacob artfully walked away with the blessings of the firstborn son. However, the outcome of that fateful day was not determined when Isaac ate of Jacob's venison but rather when Esau ate of Jacob's stew (see Genesis 27:25 and 25:33-34).

Oh how well I understand the lamentation of Esau when he realized the magnitude of his sin:

And Esau said unto his father, Hast thou but one blessing, my father? Bless me, even me also, O my father. And Esau lifted up his voice, and wept (Genesis 27:38).

Esau's sentiments mirrored my own. As I would woefully contemplate the sinful depths to which I'd sunk, my heart would consistently cry out, *O Lord, is there still forgiveness for me, my Father? Do you still love me? Can you still use me?* But rarely did my mouth utter the questions in my heart for fear of what the answers would be. Had God been the God of religion that had been so often presented to me in my youth, perhaps my fears would have been valid. But I was soon to learn that God was nothing like I imagined Him to be.

The things that I will be sharing about the love of God in this chapter are bound to offend the religious mind. So often, religion has depicted a God who is intolerant of the slightest imperfection in people. *Oh sure, He'll forgive you once or twice, but you'd better not push it buddy.* Religion has consistently peddled a message of condemnation, hoping to avert the sinner from his way. But what religion fails to understand is that it is often condemnation that aids a sinner on his journey. At any rate, in times of wrongdoing, we have learned to avoid God when in fact He is the very one we need.

Nevertheless, I am also aware that not everyone will be offended by what I am saying. There are those of you who absolutely crave an encounter with the love of God. You are just hoping that there is something more to God than judgment and intolerance. You, my friend, are the one in whom I am most interested. I want to show you that the love of God will always manifest itself when you need it the most, especially right in the midst of your sin perpetrated by your own evil heart. I want to also show you that the love of God is invincible. Do you find that hard to believe? Think of my own situation. I had plunged to the depths of sin. And by encountering the love of God, I was brought wonderfully back into the joyous presence of God, once again to exercise complete authority over the devil. From death to life. From bondage to dominion. From sin to righteousness. And all through the love of God. In the end, even my own sin, when I yielded to the love of God, could not destroy me. Is that not invincible?

When I write to you of the love of God, I am not simply reiterating the words of some sermon I heard. I am not merely giving you the Word of God on the subject, though surely that would be enough. I am writing to you from tried experience. I know the love of God because I have run—no, crashed head on!—into it, and have emerged a changed person as a result of it. Transformed: like a caterpillar after metamorphosis has enabled it to soar as a butterfly. Changed spirit, soul, and body! Strengthened! Peaceful, with a zest for life. Gone are my inhibitions towards God, my "...fearful looking for...judgment and fiery indignation" (Hebrews 10:27). The love of God has freed me to live real life, the abundant life of John 10:10. And I prophesy that as you read these pages, you too will experience the transforming power of God's love. Expect to be changed!

At the time, I did not understand why God was so eager to manifest His love on my behalf and bring me out of my situation of bondage. But later when I began to learn about covenant, I realized that God's response to my sin was the only appropriate one for a covenant-keeping God. Allow me to explain. Through the shed blood of Jesus, representative of God and man, God cut a covenant with Jesus on my behalf. When I accepted Jesus as my Lord and Savior, I accepted the covenant, and God and I became covenant partners. Consider with me the following scripture:

And we know that all things work together for the good to them that love God, to them who are the called according to His purpose (Romans 8:28).

I am in covenant with God, and so I love Him, and I am called according to His purpose. So when I became once again entangled with homosexuality, God was compelled by covenant to deliver me from this sin, to restore all homosexuality stole from me, and to completely turn things around for me. You see: I was not merely a sinner. I was a covenant person trapped in the camp of Satan, though I had foolishly wandered there myself. If God had given His Son for me when I was a sinner completely separated from Him, would He do less now that I was vitally connected to Him through covenant? Romans 8:32 says it all:

He that spared not his own Son, but delivered him up for us all, how shall he not with him also freely give us all things?

My deliverance was a sure thing, and if I had known then what I know now, it would have been immediate.

So God responds to me, and to you, through covenant. And the way He operates that covenant is by love. Therefore in my situation, his objective was deliverance. His method: love. Covenant love is one of the most powerful forces available to us as Christians. God's love is agape, or unconditional. This means that God, apart from any merit on our part, is compelled to do whatever is necessary to bring us whatever help we need in the time of trouble. He is compelled only because He loves.

It is compassion that moves Him to action. So God is not sitting around trying to determine what our punishment will be. He's not holding out so that we will learn from our trouble. No, a thousand times no! He is busy devising and implementing plans of deliverance. His desire is that we stand in this dark world as shining examples of the saving and transforming power of God. Oh how available that power becomes when only we yield!

When I think of God's dealings with me during this dark time of homosexuality, I am reminded of the words of the ancient prophet, Isaiah:

A bruised reed shall he not break, and the smoking flax shall he not quench: he shall bring forth judgment unto truth (Isaiah 42:3).

God knows I was a bruised reed. I was terribly disappointed in myself as well as disillusioned about spiritual matters. I was very near the breaking point. In the margin of my Bible, the word *smoking* is translated *dimly lit*. That term along with *bruised reed* described me precisely. In my depression, I reasoned that if I could not resist homosexuality as a Spirit-filled believer, then what hope had I of ever being free? As far as I could tell, there were no more alternatives for me. I had tried everything, even God, and failed miserably. Not only was I a dimly lit flax, but also I was quickly becoming extinguished.

But God knew how to handle me. He knew that I would crack at the least provocation, and so He was kind and gentle. I must admit though that I was somewhat puzzled by His attitude. It did not jive with what I had learned about Him as a child growing up under the tutelage of religion. I fully expected God to abandon me now that I was once again under the influence of sin. This is the way I learned it: I was supposed to repent; I was supposed to stop sinning; I was supposed to get myself out of this mess, and then God would resume his relationship with me. But that's just not the way it worked.

It is difficult to refute experience, especially when the experience is your own. I do not agree that experience is always the best teacher or even a necessary teacher. In fact, experience can sometimes be a conveyor of error. Nevertheless, when that experience confirms the Word of God, it can be trusted. In essence, God never terminated His relationship with me. On the contrary, He used that relationship to bring me to a place of lasting victory. I thought it odd, but God wanted to spend time with me, and He was always talking to me. It was hard, however, for me to accept His presence. Whenever God would show up, I would retreat in guilt and shame. You see: He was approaching me with love and mercy while I was approaching Him with an attitude of condemnation. As a result, there was no connection between Him and me, and I was unable to take advantage of the deliverance He brought with Him.

But His words! I could not resist His words. They were gentle, kind, soothing, comforting and full of promise. In spite of myself, I was drawn to them. I was one sheep—lost though I was—who knew the voice of his Shepherd. I kept hearing words. And I knew from whence they sprang. And I wanted to hear them. They would eventually usher me to the place where I could receive the love and mercy that God so untiringly offered me. There are four different occasions that I have included here that show how God, through gentle words, manifested his love on my behalf. As a result, I experienced firsthand the fulfillment of Isaiah 42:3:

> **A bruised reed shall he not break, and the smoking flax shall he not quench...**

At a Bus Stop

I was visiting my sister in Tampa. I don't know how it happened that I ended up at a bus stop. Perhaps, my sister had asked me to run an errand. Or maybe, I just wanted to take a tour of the town. At any rate, while I was waiting for a bus, I began to think about my life. I wondered how I had gravitated so far from God and if there were any hope of return. Accusatory thoughts assailed my mind, and I found the burden of guilt and shame almost impossible to bear. I simply dropped my head in despair.

Although my disposition was dark and stormy, the day was bright and windless. But suddenly, and seemingly out of nowhere, a wind began to blow. It seemed to encircle me, blowing gently around me. I felt as though it was blowing right through me. And then in my spirit, I heard the following words: "Don't worry about it. Everything is going to be alright." And then as quickly as it came, the wind was gone. And gone also, at least for the moment, was the hopelessness that so pervaded my soul. With words of love, God had replaced my despair with an expectation of deliverance.

He's A God of Faith!

On another occasion, I was sitting in my front yard. Again, I was going through about the direction my life had taken. I am amazed even now that, in my state of utter defeat, I was able to discern the voice of God. Nevertheless, I could detect the voice of God breaking defiantly though gently through my despair. I could live a million years and never forget what He said: "Robert, I expect you to be a man of faith."

To that I replied rather despondently, "I know Lord." And then I thought, *Oh well, here it comes. Finally, He is fed up with me. Finally, I have pushed Him too far. He is getting ready to let me have it.* The words that God spoke next, however, revealed to me how little I knew about the character of God.

"But I would not expect you to be anything I am not. I expect you to be a man of faith because I am a God of faith. And as a God of faith, I see you through eyes of faith. I don't see you as a homosexual, but I see you as a man of God that lives in victory over sin. I don't see you like you are; I see you the way you are going to be."

What? I couldn't believe it! Where was the angry, vindictive God of my childhood? I fully expected to feel the brunt of His wrath for my sins. After all, didn't I deserve it? I mean: had He not taken the trouble to free me from sin's control once? And there I lay, wallowing in the muck of homosexuality, like a dog returning to its vomit. And yet, God was saying to me that He didn't even see me as a sinner.

Of course, I realize now that God was trying to get across to me a principle of faith—believing before seeing—that would have brought me immediate deliverance from homosexuality. But I simply could not grasp it. It was too inconsistent with my way of thinking. However, those words did buoy me with hope. And I was finally beginning to understand one crucial fact: that God still genuinely cared for me. Again, God had spoken words of love to me, on-time, purpose-filled words: words that were gradually and definitely pulling me from the depth of sin, much like a toll truck pulls a car from wreckage.

Not Beyond Use

It had been a while since I had seen the inside of a church. But a van had canvassed the neighborhood looking for people that wanted to go to church. I pushed past my guilt and shame, boarded the van, and was soon headed for a church that I had never even heard of before. It was an extraordinary service. Every part of it, however, was a painful reminder of how things used to be. The praise was energetic but genuine. The people positively glowed as they lifted their hands to God in worship. Oh, it was clear that these people knew and loved their God. Their peace and joy, however, only made me more remorseful of my current predicament.

Still, I was absolutely mesmerized by the preaching. It wasn't just his style. It wasn't just his understanding of the Word of God. It wasn't just his confidence in the Word that he preached. But it was rather all these things and more that spun for me a web of wishful thinking. I wished that I were right with God. I wished that I could be that confident about the things of God. But more than anything else, I longed intensely to still be of use to God. Had I gone too far beyond the sweeping reach of God's love? Had I strayed too long from the sheepfold? Had I turned a deaf ear one time too many to the Shepherd's persistent call? My heart ached with agony that it was perhaps too late for me.

But God, being the covenant God of love that He is, could not allow such thoughts to go unchallenged. But God, eager that He is to pierce the darkness of Satan's lies with the light of His love, spoke directly into my befuddled heart. He said slowly and deliberately as if emphasizing each word: *I will use you yet*.

Now that did it! What audacious love! God dared to announce to me, a practicing homosexual—loathsome in the eyes of others and even my own—that He had definite plans to use me for His service. Oh how willing He was to ease any despair that I had heaped upon my soul, despair I had accepted as my just deserts. Oh how He must love me to declare me a treasure while I was still in the midst of my sin. I was overcome with emotion. I sobbed uncontrollably.

Rejected of Men, Accepted of God

It was a nightmare to end all nightmares. I was in a room full of other men. I was involved in some kind of work project that was for men only. I didn't like socializing with other men because I knew that heterosexual men despise homosexual men—or at least, that had been my experience. Though I felt this was a justified emotion on the part of heterosexual men, it did not make it easy to deal with them. Before I took the job, I knew that I would be subjected to angry looks and relentless jeering. I knew also that I would be a veritable outcast.

I couldn't have been more right about or less prepared for what I experienced when I began working with these men. I never retaliated, however, because I felt I deserved everything they dished out. It still hurt though. It hurt that they didn't like me. It hurt that they made fun of me. It hurt that they wanted absolutely nothing to do with me. I was categorically ostracized. Nobody wanted to be around me.

Did I say *nobody*? Oh was I in for a pleasant surprise. One day during a break, I was sitting in a corner brooding over my lack of friends. I looked around the room and observed as my co-workers chatted happily with each other. They seemed to be affirming for each other the most basic of sociological needs: that of belonging. But I sat alone. I tried to act tough, but there was no denying that I longed for the benefit of their company. And that is when the voice of God broke through my loneliness. I wasn't completely surprised though. By now, even in the brokenness of sin, I had learned that God was always interested in speaking to me when I was troubled. Still, I could never have predicted what He was about to say: "Don't worry about it. You can hang around me."

What an awesome invitation when you think of it. Here men, themselves sinful, had judged me unworthy of their company. And yet perfect, sinless, matchless God had invited me into His very presence. *Man, doesn't He know what I am?* I was a homosexual, and yet God said that I could hang around Him! Alas, it was enough for me. God had offered me His love and for the moment, nobody else seemed to matter. For nothing can more effectively snuff out the pain of man's rejection than the unconditional acceptance of God.

I have endeavored in these pages to convey to you the love of God that is available to you even when you are undeserving. I hope that I have convinced you that God is eager to love you. I hope that you are now willing to take advantage of His love. I am certainly glad I did. My experience with the love of God, however, does not end here. Read on with me into the next chapter and discover how God's love finally brought me to lasting deliverance.

CHAPTER NINE

INVINCIBLE LOVE
PART TWO

One of the things that Americans cherish most is freedom. We have at least two national holidays set aside that commemorate the men that have fought and died in the name of freedom. We take pride in the fact that no one can tell us what to do. We can do whatever we want whenever we want and however we want. And through the years, our country has sustained ideological changes that have catapulted it into a chaotic, free-for-all, freethinking society. Freedom has become our one virtue, and it is a virtue that we will have at any cost. How far we've progressed, or shall I say regressed, that we can burn the American flag without fear of repercussion or even a twinge of conscience.

This is not my call for patriotism, nor is it my plug for repressive authority. I simply want to point out that the characteristic independent thinking of secular society has no place among those who wish to be pleasing to God. I learned a long time ago that the best way to get along with God is to just do what He says. Although God will not force your hand, He is not at all shy about telling you what to do. I often think of God as bossy. For sure, a person bent on having things his own way will always clash with God. God simply will not bend to the will of man because He always knows best. It is we who must constantly realign our own wills so that they fit with God's will.

Indeed, God is a God of mercy who is motivated by love as my own story reveals. But He is also a God of truth. Even though God was gentle with me, He never changed His mind about homosexuality. Regardless of how devastated I was, God never sought to comfort me by relaxing His stance against homosexuality. During these times, in all my dealings with God, it was always clear to me that homosexuality is a sin, and that my only recourse was to discontinue my practice of it.

But I was never once alone, even though I didn't always know it. From the moment that I ventured back into homosexuality, God sprang into action on my behalf with deliverance as His goal. His gentle expressions of love were just a means to that end. But there is no sustained deliverance without instruction. And it is by consistently following the instructions of God that we happen upon the road to freedom. But because we are often shortsighted, we fail to grasp the rationale behind God's instructions. Consequently, we balk at the very instructions that are designed to bring us out of captivity. I am here reminded of one such incidence.

It was the spring of 1989. If spring, as celebrated in poetic literature, is a time of renewal, then certainly my life was out of season. I sat on my bed contemplating the sorrows of my existence. I had lost my second job in less than a week, and I had no money. I'd previously had an experience in homelessness, and I was now worried about repeating it. To make matters worse, I was still enslaved by homosexuality. As I sat there, nursing a heart heavy with despair, one question prevailed in my thinking: *What am I going to do? What am I going to do?*

Now you must understand that I didn't pray. I didn't ask God for His input. I was too consumed by worry to even think of God. No one was further from my thoughts. But God does not sit quietly by waiting for permission to speak. So often, He would speak and then you can choose to do whatever you want with what He says. This time He said to me, "Join the Army." It is still amusing to me how God is always emphatic and decisive about what He says. He never makes suggestions!

Now the voice I heard was not audible, but it was unmistakably God's. In fact, I was so sure that I was hearing from God that I spoke right up, "The Army? God, I don't like the Army!" I was emphatic, not at all acquiescent. God had grown quiet at my thoughtless retort. This concerned me a little, so I promptly shut my mouth.

However, my mind would not be so easily shut down. It eagerly took up where my mouth left off. *The Army? What kind of sense does that make? I could have stayed in school. I would have graduated by now, and perhaps would have a Master's Degree. I would have a good job and everything would be all right. He took me out of school. And now He wants me to join the Army. I just don't understand.*

My mind carried on in that vein for some time but eventually grew quiet. It was then God had the opportunity to speak to me again, "This will not be a career move for you. But there is something that I have for you. And you will not get it unless you join the Army."

I couldn't possibly imagine what the Army had to offer me, but I also knew that God would never change His mind. I knew that there were only two alternatives: to obey or to disobey. And I knew that disobedience would only bring me more unrest. And so it was that with a little trepidation, I paid a visit to the recruiting office the very next day.

When I arrived, I noticed that the Army and Air Force offices were adjacently located. It was then that I was struck with a brilliant idea. I would join the Air Force. I had heard about the Air Force. In fact, a good friend of my sister was enlisted in the Air Force. I had concluded from contact with her that perhaps the Air Force was not a bad deal. They had first class facilities, good food and good people. They valued education, and allegedly, their basic training was considerably more bearable. Yes of course, when God said Army, He must have meant Air Force. After all, He knew of my aversion for the Army. And surely, God wouldn't require me to do anything that I didn't want to do.

I walked into the Air Force office and promptly sat down to an interview with one of the recruiters. He told me all about the Air Force including its emphasis on education. He assured me that I would likely be able to complete my degree while enlisted with the Air Force. So far, his speech confirmed my good feelings. It soon became my turn to tell him about myself. I left nothing out including a minor run-in I'd had with the law. When I finished, he told me that he would have to do a more thorough legal investigation and would be contacting me later concerning the status of my enlistment. I stood up, shook his hand and walked out the door feeling somewhat dejected. Instinctively, I knew that he would not be getting back with me.

When I stepped out the door, I was immediately greeted by the voice of God: "I said Army!" At that, I stepped through the door of the Army Recruiting Office. After an interview and completing the necessary paperwork, I was scheduled to take the ASVAB, an aptitude test required for entry into the military. I passed the ASVAB, and within weeks after hearing God's instructions to "go Army," I was flying the friendly skies to Fort Jackson, South Carolina to begin basic training.

At Fort Jackson, I became quickly acquainted with military life. The first couple of weeks were really difficult, as I tried to adjust to the being constantly yelled at, awakened before dawn and subjected to strenuous activities. In no time at all, however, my adjustment was complete, and I was really beginning to like the Army. Nonetheless, other than a steady paycheck and job security, I still did not understand why God had been so adamant about me enlisting in the Army.

From Fort Jackson, I went to Fitzsimons Army Medical Center in Aurora, Colorado. There, I would spend almost a year in additional training to prepare for a permanent position with the Army. I arrived in Colorado just a little excited. I have always enjoyed traveling to new places, but perhaps my excitement could not entirely be attributed to my change in geographical location. It had been more than a couple of months since my last homosexual encounter. I knew that I wasn't delivered, but still hope lingered. Here I was: in a new place and with a new job. Could it be that I might have a new life as well, free from homosexuality? I pushed past the thought—wishful, it seemed to me. I was content for the moment just to have a reprieve from the cruel dominion of sin.

However, God had something more permanent in mind for me. The following Saturday, I boarded a city bus and commenced my search for a Christian bookstore. I wanted to replenish my collection of gospel music cassette tapes (prior to the era of compact discs). I saw a mini shopping area and spotted what I thought was a Christian bookstore. Exiting the bus, I walked over to the *store*. There were two gentlemen standing in front engaged in what seemed to be idle chatter. From them, I ascertained that the place I had mistaken for a store was actually a storefront Pentecostal church. After giving me directions to the nearest bookstore and learning that I was new to their city, they invited me to church.

Now Faith Christian Center Church was bursting at the seams with people and, in a greater way, the Spirit of God. The atmosphere was charged with excitement. I had never before experienced such an awesome time of praise and worship. Not only were the musicians and singers extremely talented, but they also seemed to be alive with God Himself. Their praise was loud, joyful and uninhibited. Their worship was sweet, soothing and inviting of the very presence of God.

Such preaching as I had never heard before followed the praise and worship. I listened with rapt attention, accompanied by excited gestures, to every word that Pastor Leon Emerson spoke. It excited me to hear about God in this way. According to Pastor Emerson, God was a God of love and compassion. He delighted in destroying the bondages that come into the lives of so many people. The God that Pastor Emerson sang-preached about was both willing and able to deliver me from the sin that had pervaded my soul for so long.

And yet when he extended an invitation for prayer, I remained stubbornly at my seat. My calm exterior veiled the struggle that raged inside me. I knew that I desperately needed prayer, but pride held me back. Because of my overtly feminine mannerisms, I reasoned that everyone present would guess what dreadful thing necessitated my trip to the altar. But then again, why did I care so much about the opinions of others? I was so tired of hurting, so tired of the condemnation of sin. So tired of constantly falling short of the glory of God. What I needed was a life-changing encounter with God. So why couldn't

I just walk the few feet to the front of the sanctuary where I could have such an encounter? I simply could not bear the shame of everybody knowing.

I finally did end up at the altar, though not for myself. I accompanied someone else in order to provide moral support, or so I thought. While waiting at the altar, I suddenly became excited and began to dance. This got Pastor Emerson's attention. Before I knew it, he was upon me with hands heavy with the anointing. As he prayed, he said something to me that I will never forget: "Young man, it's good to be excited, but you need to be delivered." As he continued to pray, I simply surrendered, more from embarrassment than from a genuine desire to be free.

I left the church that afternoon with two opposite emotions competing for my endorsement. The word *bittersweet* comes to mind. There were three things that I absolutely knew. First, I knew that I was delivered from homosexuality as a result of Pastor Emerson's prayer. I had not heard any thunders from heaven or a loud voice within, but I knew that I was finally and forever free. Secondly, I knew that I was also embarrassed by what happened to me at Now Faith. And I simply did not have the heart to return. This troubled me because I also knew that Now Faith was an excellent church and regular attendance there would help me sustain deliverance.

All those encounters with the love of God had taught me one thing: I could trust God. I couldn't talk to Pastor Emerson or any of the members of Now Faith about my feelings, as they were all strangers to me. However, by now, I trusted enough in the love of God to know that I could confide in Him. And so I did, "Lord, I know I need to go back to Now Faith. But the truth is that I am too ashamed to go back. And if you don't help me get over this shame, then I will never return."

I am convinced that nobody understands you like God. And no one is more eager to help you than God. Most people would probably have belittled my emotions and demanded that I get on with life. After all, God had delivered me, hadn't He? So I should just quit my bellyaching! But God would design a sort of object lesson to help me get over those emotions. While I was waiting in a checkout line, I was suddenly prompted by God to look into my wallet. When I did so, I discovered that I had less money than I thought and certainly not enough to pay for all my merchandise. I returned some of the items to stock and got back into the checkout line. While waiting for the clerk to ring up my goods, I was again confronted with the voice of God:

"Robert, I am not interested in embarrassing you. I know you, and I know what embarrasses you and what does not. If I were solely interested in embarrassing you, then I would not have prompted you to look in your wallet. I did so because I knew you would have been embarrassed had the discovery been made at the cash register. It was not my intention to embarrass you at Now Faith. I only wanted to set you free from homosexuality. I would have chosen another way, but you left me no alternative."

The more I thought about it, the more I realized that God had a point. How many times had He wooed me with gentle words of love in an effort to set me free? How many times could I have walked up to some brother in private, shared my plight with him, and then requested his prayers? How many times had I strayed from churches out of a fear of being found out? How many times had I preferred the mire of self-pity above the fertile pasture of God's love? And that fateful morning at Now Faith: how He had pleaded with me to go to the altar of my own volition!

So all that time I had been entrapped by homosexuality, God had endeavored to set me free. All His many attempts perpetrated on my behalf had simply been returned to sender. Finally, He did the only thing left to do. He set me up to be confronted in a place where there would be no escape. And even then, He did so only after ensuring that I would be strong enough—actually secure enough in His love—to handle such a confrontation. And so Love had done it! Love had succeeded in bringing me face to face with the anointed purpose of Jesus Christ:

> **The Spirit of the Lord is upon me, because He has anointed me to preach the gospel to the poor; He has sent me to heal the brokenhearted, to preach deliverance to the captives, and recovering of sight to the blind, to set at liberty them that are bruised (Luke 4:18).**

I was at last free. More free than I had been bound! From that moment on, I had no problem being at Now Faith. In fact, I was so grateful for what God had done that I couldn't care less about what others thought. I returned to Now Faith, camped out on the front pew, and praised God vigorously at every service.

But now that I was free, I wanted to stay free. I could not bear another repeat of my past. With the deliverance from homosexuality came a clarity and strength of mind. I knew this time that I had to do something to maintain my freedom. As I sought God about it, He began to show me how to stay free. In the remainder of this chapter, I would like to share with you three things that have kept me free from homosexuality for all these years.

1. Become Covenant-Minded.

One of the first things I had to realize was that I am in covenant with God. And love is the motivating force behind that covenant. Therefore, God would always respond to me in love. I never needed to fear disappointing God when I made mistakes. I only needed to bring all my concerns to Him and know that He is able to deal with each one of them.

When David cried out to God because of the oppression of ungodly men, God's response to His covenant friend was immediate and powerful:

> **The earth shook and trembled; the foundations also of the hills moved and were shaken, because He was wroth...He sent out His arrows, and scattered them; and shot out lightnings, and discomfited them. He delivered me from my strong enemy, and from them, which hated me (Psalms 18:7, 14, 17).**

The Bible says that we have a better covenant established upon better promises (see Hebrews 8:6). If God moved so powerfully against David's enemies, will He do less for me, even if, and especially if, the culprit is sin? How equipped I became to stand against the temptation of homosexuality when I understood that my Covenant-Friend would always be there to back me up.

Jesus is the Mediator of the Covenant.

I had to realize that without Jesus, there is no covenant relationship with God. But through Jesus, I had access to relationship with God. And through Jesus, I had access to everything necessary for godly living. As I concentrated on this truth, I no longer tried to be adequate in myself but placed my dependency completely in the righteousness of Jesus. So then when I did fall short in any area, I was no longer devastated as before. I simply got up, repented and kept right on going.

The covenant between David and Jonathan illustrates this point beautifully (Read II Samuel 9). After Jonathan's death in battle, David was compelled by covenant love to extend goodness to someone in Jonathan's family. Through inquiry, David discovered that Jonathan had a surviving son, Mephibosheth. After summoning him from Lodebar, David restored to him all the possessions that pertained to Saul. He also commanded Ziba and his fifteen sons and twenty servants to become servants of Mephibosheth. Talk about rags to riches. Mephibosheth had been an outcast in the land of Lodebar, without possessions, crippled in his feet and cowering in fear from an imagined threat from David. In an instant, however, he had become as rich as his grandfather, was commissioned to sit at the king's table and had been given 36 servants to boot. Check out Mephibosheth's response to the king's generosity:

> **And he bowed himself, and said, what is thy servant that thou should look upon such a dead dog as I am? (II Samuel 9:8).**

If you read the next verse, you can plainly see that David paid absolutely no attention to Mephibosheth's words. Why? Because David was honoring a covenant that he made with Jonathan. And the covenant required him to be good to Jonathan's relatives. So it didn't matter if Mephibosheth was a dead dog or a live cat. When David looked upon Mephibosheth, he saw Jonathan.

I discovered that this was exactly God's perspective of me. Because of covenant, when He saw me, He saw Jesus. He did not reckon any of my sins to my account. So then when the devil tried to use my past against me, I concentrated on my present state of righteousness with God through Christ

Jesus. When I was delivered from homosexuality, I was also delivered from my "dead dog" mentality. And this was the very mentality the devil had used to bring homosexuality back into my life. With it gone, the devil was absolutely powerless against me.

2. Accept God's Forgiveness.

I discovered this point to be absolutely crucial to my freedom. If I could not accept God's forgiveness, then I could not stay free. We must forgive ourselves, and let go of our past. How utterly futile it is to harbor guilt when the God of the universe has declared you guiltless. To what higher authority could you appeal? I John 1:9 helps us accept the forgiveness of God:

> **If we confess our sins, he is faithful and just to forgive us our sins, and to cleanse us from all unrighteousness.**

Of course, one of the first steps in walking in forgiveness is to confess our sins. But even after confession, so many people are still held captive by guilty feelings. This is so dangerous because it breeds condemnation. And believe me: condemnation makes it almost impossible for you to remain free.

There are two words in this scripture that are particularly important. First of all, we understand that God is **faithful** to forgive. That means that God will forgive every time. His forgiveness is something we can depend on. Secondly, God is **just** to forgive. To be just is to be right, not merciful but right! So when God forgives us, He is doing the right thing.

Forgiveness is the right thing because it is a covenant provision to be used when I mess up. The covenant itself is a covenant of grace and mercy. But the provisions of the covenants are our Blood-bought (not earned, not deserved) rights. In other words, if I meet the condition for forgiveness—that is, if I repent, and I forgive others—then I have a right to be forgiven. Again, I emphasize that the right is not earned or deserved; it is provided through the Blood of Jesus. That sounds strange because we don't often think of forgiveness as a right. But it is because it is a provision of the covenant. As Christians, we have a right to the provisions of the covenant as long as we meet the conditions of the covenant. So when the devil came around to condemn me about wrongdoing, I would hit him over the head with this scripture and simply stand on my right to be forgiven. I learned that forgiveness belongs to me, just as much as salvation, healing or prosperity.

3. Be Vocal About Your Deliverance.

I learned that I could not expect to stay free if I was not willing to be vocal about my deliverance. This goes back to our discussion on thoughts, words and images. When the devil would again bring thoughts of homosexuality to me, I could not afford to simply shrug them away. No! I had to speak to those thoughts, thus uprooting them with my words. I never gave the devil the opportunity to tempt me again. Because at the slightest thought, I would open my mouth boldly and sometimes angrily against the devil, he never again was able to build up a stronghold of homosexuality in my mind. Below is a sample of what I might say: "No devil, I will have none of your thoughts of homosexuality. I know that they are not my own, and you will not trick me into believing they are. I know that God has already delivered me from homosexuality. I remember the month, the day and the time. God has redeemed me from the power of darkness and has translated me into the kingdom of His dear Son. Homosexuality has no more power over me. I am not whimsically in your control. I know that if I don't want to succumb to homosexuality then I don't have to. And since I don't want to, then I will not!"

And then I would begin to praise God for that deliverance. The devil doesn't usually stick around for praise and worship. I did this over and over again until my mind was purged of any homosexual tendencies. I never did experience any more feelings of homosexuality because I never would allow any thought to take root in my mind.

Besides all that, I finally realized that I belong to God, not to the devil. It is none of his business what goes on with me, even when I sin. If I were to sin—regardless of the sin—I'd go to God and in humility accept whatever comes from His hand. But I won't, even for a moment, tolerate a word from the devil about any of my mistakes. You too can get free and stay free. If you are born again, you have what it takes. If you are not, then you can get born again and get what it takes. Decide now to be forever free! Surely you know by now that the love of God is available to get you there.

Chapter Ten

GOD, THE MATCHMAKER

Remember that I told you that God instructed me to join the Army. Remember also that He told me that He had something for me that I could only get if I joined the Army. Well that something, I was sure, was my deliverance. But God was not about to stop there. He was about to deliver something to me that would change my life forever: a good thing, baby!

I had been convinced for years now that marriage was a part of God's will for my life. However, because I had been so battered by homosexuality, I concluded that marriage was still a long ways off. Before I left Florida for basic training, I had decided that I would be well into my forties before finally settling down. I figured that it would take me that long to be healed from the wounds of homosexuality. Furthermore, I was sure that any woman would require me to have experienced years of freedom from homosexuality before extending to me her hand in marriage.

Yet when I landed in Denver, I had the strange sensation that somewhere within the confines of that city was my wife. I was not yet delivered from homosexuality, and so I dismissed it as just a thought. But after I gained freedom from homosexuality, God began to deal with me about marriage. I could hardly believe that God would propose marriage so soon after my deliverance. And one day, I found myself voicing this concern out loud: "God, do you really think that I am ready for marriage." To which he abruptly replied, "If I say you're ready, then you are ready!"

Well, that was enough to convince me, and despite my earlier misgivings, I became increasingly excited about the prospect of marriage. I still had some apprehension. After all, what did I know about women? I had never in my life had any romantic dealings with women. I mean, what would I say to one? How would I manage the courage to ask one on a date? And what would I do once I got her to say yes—to a date, that is? The more I thought about my ignorance about women, the more nervous I became. However, I was soon to discover that even men that have been heterosexual all their lives know very little about women. I reasoned that I was at an advantage because at least, I was willing to admit my ignorance. That way, God had a better chance of teaching me something.

As time progressed, the sensation to get married returned and even intensified. I finally realized that God was getting me ready for marriage soon. I really got excited, perhaps a little too excited. I began to try to figure out whom God had chosen. I knew she was at Now Faith, and as I would look around from face to face, I would wonder: *Is it her, Lord? Is it her?* During one such interrogation, I was sure God had answered in the affirmative.

I'll call her *Tammy*. She was beautiful and petite, with red hair. She had spunk and style. She was also filled with the Holy Spirit and appeared serious about her relationship with God. I must admit that I was infatuated with her. I thought to myself: *surely she is the one*. But two things were wrong. First, I couldn't get God to confirm my suspicion that she was His choice. Secondly, she was not at all interested in me. Still hope lingered.

The day would come, however, when God would leave nothing to uncertainty. It was late September 1989. Our church was hosting a series of evangelistic services. The guest speaker was a lady of small stature. But what she lacked in stature she more than compensated for in presence. She had a forceful and authoritative voice. She had a flash of determination in her eye that was somewhat akin to anger. I was sure that every demon in hell was afraid of her.

One evening during the revival, she spoke about completion. She believed that God was going to complete, or finish, some things in our lives. I could think of a few things that needed to be completed for me. And so I listened excitedly as she continued her sermon. More than occasionally, I demonstrated my approval with loud shouts.

At the conclusion of her sermon, she took up an offering, during which she requested that people give $77. She informed us that this amount was symbolic because seven was the number of completion. Well, $77 was about all the money I had, but God convinced me to give it. I walked over to the offering basket and deposited my check for $77. As I returned to my seat, I heard God say, "Your completion is on the way." I don't think I knew then that He meant my wife!

At the end of the service on the last day of the revival, my soon to be wife and I and two other guys were standing about in a sort of circle, engaged in lively conversation. We talked exclusively about God—that He was good; that we appreciated His goodness and that we were excited about Him and wanted to commit our lives to Him. At one point, I was speaking while looking around the circle at each face. Suddenly, it was as though time momentarily stood still. As my eyes focused on Kimberly, I was surprised by an old familiar voice, "She is the one." I knew that voice, and I knew exactly what He meant. God was saying that Kimberly was to be my wife.

Well, Kimberly may have been God's choice, but she certainly was not mine. I had not provided God with a list, but I knew what I desired in a woman. Don't get me wrong: Kimberly was and still is a very beautiful woman. But I wanted a woman with long hair and long fingernails. I wanted a woman that adorned herself lavishly with make-up, jewelry and form-fitting clothes. Of all the women at New Faith that met these qualifications—with their weaves and fake fingernails—God had chosen the one woman that didn't. In fact, Kimberly was the one woman that most of the Now Faith congregation could not see in a romantic relationship.

Besides that, I didn't know her, didn't know anything about her. I barely knew her name. But God would listen to none of my objections, and I knew that He could not be swayed otherwise. And so I asked Kimberly out for a picnic lunch and a trip to the zoo. Kimberly and I had opposing work schedules, so two weeks passed before we made good on our plans.

But there was still the situation with *Tammy*. I really liked her and she seemed more my type. I really didn't understand why she could not be the one. (It didn't dawn on me that the fact that she was not interested in me was reason enough). After all, she was born-again, Spirit-filled and serious about God. Wasn't that all that mattered? Absolutely not! Our choice of mate needs to be God's choice.

I came close to repeating the mistake that so many men before me had made: choosing a wife based solely on physical appeal. I did, however, have a little something going for me. Because of my past, I was not at all confident in my ability to choose a wife. Consequently, I looked to God for guidance in making such a crucial choice. It just so happened that His choice was not my choice.

God, however, has always had a way of bringing me around. He simply said, "Tammy is like Ishmael to you; but Kimberly is Isaac." In other words, God was informing me, in a way that I could understand, that as Isaac was for Abraham, Kimberly was for me the fulfillment of promise. She would be able to understand and accept me, past and all. Any choice other than Kimberly could invite long-term and tragic consequences. I was convinced.

The day would arrive when Kimberly and I would commence the first phase of our love connection: the big date! (At least, it was big for me). During our date, I was fraught with nervous energy. I knew that God had chosen Kimberly to be my wife, but had He remembered to tell her? If not, how was I going to break the news to her? And even if she did know, how would I even broach the subject? The pressure was on. I chose the subtle approach. I chattered incessantly about this woman that God had chosen to be my wife. The plan was to say something that would jar her memory about what God had said to her about me, if indeed, God had said anything at all. At this point, I just wasn't sure. I must have been too subtle, however, because by that afternoon, after almost nonstop chatter, Kimberly was none the wiser. I found out later that she actually thought I was talking about another woman.

Nevertheless, I still enjoyed our date. Kimberly was scheduled to attend an altar worker's meeting at our church that evening. An altar worker is someone who assists the pastor in praying for people. Anyway, I expressed a desire to accompany her to this meeting, and she agreed to pick me up around seven (I didn't own a car at the time). At the meeting, I was somewhat distracted. I was sure that I had heard from God. Kimberly definitely was to be my wife. But so far, I had not been able to convey this to her. And I was fresh out of ideas. I feared the night would pass into oblivion without the two of us ever making that connection.

But I should have known that God would have the last word and that His word would be the one that would clinch the deal. After the meeting, Kimberly and I stood near the exit of the church, engaged in a friendly conversation with Sister Kate Emerson. Sister Kate was actually one of Pastor Emerson's sisters. She is someone that Kimberly and I still admire to this day. She was just the one God needed to crack this case wide open.

Her next words were not extraordinary in and of themselves. They composed perhaps what has become one of the most commonly asked questions. On any other occasion, asked of any other person, they probably would have barely been acknowledged. But for me, they seemed to be words straight from the mouth of God. They were the words that would seal my happy fate.

Don't you think it's time for you to settle down? That was just the icebreaker we needed. Kimberly and I both began to laugh as though released from some horrible captivity. I laughed, relieved that she finally understood that we were to be together. I'm not sure why she laughed, but her laughter reinforced the reason I had laughed. And so by the end of our first date, it was final: Robert Fitzgerald Pinkney and Kimberly Salyce Lindsey were soon to be joined in holy matrimony. That statement sounded as though it belonged to a clipping for the social section of the town newspaper, or to a page yellowed and torn from a romance novel. But we knew—and were glad that we knew— that it was a realistic prediction of the rest of our lives.

The ride back to my barracks was hardly endured in silence. Kimberly and I talked untiringly about God's plans for our lives. It was hard to believe. We barely knew each other. We had not come together in the traditional way that couples are united. We were not in love with each other. In fact, we did not even prefer each other. But here we were at the end of our first date already making plans to get married. For me, it would have been frightening had I not been so sure that I had heard from God.

When we finally arrived at Fitzsimons, I was exhausted from excitement. Before bidding her farewell, I provided her some food for thought:

"I love you. Now I don't feel like I love you. In fact, it feels odd to say it. But I know I must love you because God has said that I am to marry you. And God would not give you someone that did not love you."

She agreed. We also agreed that we would date with the definite goal of getting married. Our dating would not be just another "weeding out" process. We established right then and there to pledge obedience to God's will for our lives, the least of which was marriage.

On the walk back to the barracks, I marveled that I was so willing to marry someone for whom I had no feelings. Sure I was excited. But I was excited about the idea of getting married; I was not excited about Kimberly. But still, I was determined to obey God. Before the end of the week, however, our feelings would no longer be an issue. To use an old cliché, Kimberly and I fell head over heels in love with each other. Our feelings were so profoundly and so quickly transformed that we knew that God was behind this sudden change. He had responded to our obedience. It was especially miraculous for me because I had never felt anything for any woman ever before in my life. God used this experience to teach Kimberly and me a very valuable lesson. Obedience always comes before feelings. We understood that our feelings would not always readily agree with God's instructions. But if we obeyed anyway, our feelings would always follow suit. We have endeavored since to govern our lives by that principle.

Okay, now things were going very well. We had agreed to marry each other. And we even had those feelings that so enhanced our time with each other. But there was still for me one more obstacle to overcome: my past. I always knew that I would be honest with my wife concerning my past of homosexuality. And so I knew that I would eventually have to reveal my past to Kimberly. It was only a matter of when, where and how. As I sat on my bed one afternoon, God began to deal with me about this issue. He was impressing upon me that now was the time to have a little tell-all with Kimberly.

Now God, I thought to myself, *but we have only been dating for two weeks*. But the impression was unmistakable: now was definitely the time. God explained it to me this way:

"I know that you have been dating for only a short time. But it is important for you to tell her before she becomes too emotionally attached to you. That way she can make an objective decision about whether to continue the relationship with you. She will decide to stay in the relationship. But it is fair to her that you allow her the right to make an objective decision." God was calling all the shots. I was glad for that. Because of my limited knowledge of women and the affairs of the heart, I was ill equipped to come up with such advice on my own. It was clear that God was going to show me how to do this husband-wife thing.

Kimberly and I met the next evening. We sat in her car in the parking lot adjacent to my barracks. There, we had a heart to heart talk. It would be our first shared instance of vulnerability. I was a little nervous, though, because I was the one being vulnerable. Knowing, however, that I was following the prompting of the Holy Spirit encouraged me to some extent. This would be the big night. This would be where the rubber meets the road. If we could get past this moment of revelation, then I was sure that we could do anything.

I began the conversation by informing Kimberly that I needed her to listen to me without comment. When I was finished, then she could voice her concerns, ask her questions. And then I told her all about my past experiences with homosexuality. I left nothing out, including the fact that it had only been six months since my last homosexual encounter. I opened up to her about things that I could not discuss in this book, things that I have never told another living soul. I told her all because I believed she had the right to know.

After bearing my soul, I breathed a sigh of relief. It was good to get it all out. Regardless of what her response to my exposé would be, I knew I had reached a milestone in my life. I was able to share my past with someone without cringing in guilt and shame. In the few months since my deliverance, I could tell that I had received some emotional healing as well.

Kimberly uttered only three words in response to my confessional. But they were three of the most liberating words I had ever heard. *Past is past.* And they had serious implications for my personal life and our relationship. *Past is past.* For me, they meant that I could cast out the skeletons in my closet and prepare myself for a glorious future with God through Jesus Christ. *Past is past.* They granted our relationship permission to be and to thrive against all the obstacles in its path. *Past is past.* Armed with those words, with Jesus in my heart, and Kimberly by my side, I could tread the rough waters that lay just ahead of me as I attempted to forge a new life free of homosexuality, under the watchful eyes of my self-proclaimed critics—Christians and non-Christians alike. And what a fitting way to end the last chapter of this section: indeed, past is past!

The conclusion of the matter

What a wonderful change that has transpired in my life! At this writing, Kimberly and I have been happily married for over twenty years. We have never once doubted that we are meant to be together. God has also blessed us with four children: two daughters and two sons. I have preached and ministered on various occasions and in different places. So you see: God has fulfilled the promise He made to me as a lad. And He has even greater plans for me.

It still seems amazing sometimes to think that I have metamorphosed from a wimpy, defeated homosexual boy into a stallion of a man. The proud father of four children. The capable head of my household. The passionate lover of the woman of my dreams. A covenant friend of the God of heaven. A formidable foe of the devil. Cleansed by the blood of Jesus. Kept by the Holy Spirit.

Gone forever is the pain of my past. In fact, when I remember my past, it is as though it has happened to someone else. God has so removed from me the shame, the guilt and all the negative emotions of homosexuality that I can hardly remember what it felt like to be homosexual. I can remember that it happened, but I don't remember it with emotion. In fact, my memory of the past is more a testimony to the awesome power of God to completely restore a broken life. I am absolutely and undeniably free.

I wrote this book for one reason only:

> **The Spirit of the Lord is upon me, because he hath anointed me to preach the gospel to the poor; he hath sent me to heal the brokenhearted, to preach deliverance to the captives, and recovering of sight to the blind, to set at liberty them that are bruised, To preach the acceptable year of the Lord (Luke 4:18, 19).**

The same anointing, the same power, the same love that set me free is available to set you free as well. The name of the game is freedom. Are you poor? God has freedom from poverty for you! Has sin and disappointment broken your heart? God has healing for you. Have you been taken captive by the perversions of this world, sexual or otherwise? There is certain deliverance for you. Are you physically and spiritually blind? Are you bruised? God has already awarded you recovery of all things that you have lost.

And this is the acceptable year of the Lord, the year of God's abounding favor. This is your year. This is your time of victory and freedom in every circumstance and every situation. No doubt, as you've read through the pages of this book, you've thirsted after an encounter with God, the kind that will radically change your life for the better. Determine now that you will have that encounter. Listen to the voice of God as he leads you to victory. Do whatever it talks to walk in the will of God. And you will be able to proclaim with me: "Free at last! Free at last! Thank you, Jesus for making me free at last!"

FROM *her* PERSPECTIVE

CHAPTER ONE

THE BEGINNING OF CHANGE
from her perspective

In 1989 just when the seasons began their change from summer to fall, I sensed that a change was on the horizon for me as well. Little did I know how great a change in my life I was about to experience. In II Corinthians 5:17, the Bible makes an interesting statement about change: "Therefore if any man be in Christ, he is a new creature: old things are passed away; behold all things are become new."

The truth represented in this scripture was very hard for me to believe when Robert and I started dating. I often asked myself the question: how can someone who was once involved in homosexuality be new, not just spirit new but attitude new? Little did I know back then how God was going to use Robert to change my life and thinking forever.

Before I begin to tell you the wonderful and very interesting story about how Robert and I met and how God truly blesses obedience, let me tell you a little about myself. This is necessary if you are to understand fully the reasons that the devil brought so much doubt into my mind during the course of our dating.

I grew up in Colorado as a Baptist, so much so that I thought I was born one and would surely die one. I accepted Jesus Christ as Savior at an early age. The Baptist church where I attended taught me a lot of things about God. Our church was one of the most prosperous churches in the city. During that time, there was a gentleman in attendance who was a hard worker and quite devoted to the church. He was also extremely talented. But rumor had it that he was also a homosexual. Actually, I didn't see anything wrong with him until the rumors started spreading. And that's when I found out what homosexuality really involves.

Now you could probably guess what a stir this made in the church, so much of one that he had to leave. I was hurt because he was a very nice person. I didn't understand why people made such a big deal of his sexual orientation. Of course, at the time, I did not know what the Bible had to say about homosexuality. As I got older, I encountered so many homosexuals and lesbians at school and other places that I began to wonder about my own sexual preference. However, by this time, I had learned from my church as well as the Bible that homosexuality is a sin.

Consequently, I kept running from the feelings of homosexuality. I also wanted to prove to myself that I wasn't a lesbian. I got very interested in boys. When that didn't make me feel free or take away the feelings that were growing inside, I started disliking homosexuals and lesbians altogether. I didn't want anything to do with them. In fact, I really couldn't stand them. What's more, if you had told me that one had gotten saved, I would not have believed you because as far as I was concerned, once a person is homosexual, that person is always homosexual. I felt this way because most of the homosexuals that I ran across, male and female, confessed salvation but continued practicing homosexuality. This naturally confused me because of what the Bible says about homosexuality. Somehow, the concept of a Christian homosexual was hard for me to grasp.

Then someone told me to give in to those feelings of homosexuality. Their specific advice was that if I stop resisting the feelings, then my confusion would clear up. But in the back of my head, I kept hearing that according to the Bible, homosexuality is wrong. I now know that this was the Spirit of God speaking truth to my mind to keep me away from homosexuality. Still, my feelings and consequent confusion lingered for some time. I still disliked homosexuals. I realized, of course, that my attitude towards homosexuals was wrong because the Bible teaches as much against hatred as it does against homosexuality. However, this was my only way of coping with the feelings inside me.

As time passed, I began to develop a hunger and thirst for more of the things of God. You see, besides inner turmoil, I had physical problems as well. In fact, I was very ill. For a long time, I had been suffering with epilepsy, hypoglycemia, juvenile arthritis and severe stress. Epilepsy was particularly a concern for me because it was growing in intensity. By 1988, I was having seizures about two weeks out of every month, and was going from one medication to another in a futile effort to control them. Of course, the medicine had very unpleasant side effects. Additionally, my joints ached constantly, my blood sugar levels were crazy and my stress level was beginning to threaten my mental health.

Then, in the fall of '88, the Lord led me to leave my Baptist church and join a Pentecostal church in the area. And so I did. The very first Sunday I was in attendance, Pastor Leon Emerson (pastor of Now Faith Christian Center Church) preached about divine healing. He spoke confidently of healing being the will of God for every Christian. He preached that the devil is the author of sickness and disease, not God. He said that God is the healer, not the stealer. He said that the devil comes to steal, kill and destroy, and Jesus comes to stop him!

Of course, this was all news to me, but I was so sick and so desperate for deliverance that I listened intently. In his case against sickness and disease, Pastor Emerson spoke about the epileptic boy that Jesus healed. Imagine my pleasant surprise: I didn't even know there was an epileptic boy in the Bible (see Luke 9:38-42). I know that some people disagree that this was a case of epilepsy, but after considering my own history of epilepsy, I was convinced that it was. At any rate, Pastor Emerson pointed out that the fact that Jesus healed the epileptic boy proved that God didn't afflict the boy with epilepsy. In other words, how could Jesus, who was dedicated to doing the will of the Father, undo something that God had done?

Well you know what they say—"my mama didn't raise no fool!" I was fully persuaded that God could heal me. Actually, it seemed that a light came on inside of me, and for the first time in my life, I realized God wanted me healed! I reasoned that if he could heal that boy of epilepsy, then certainly he could heal me of epilepsy. I reasoned further that if he could heal me of epilepsy, then he could heal me of hypoglycemia, arthritis and stress. So I joined that church. Later, I answered an altar call to be healed physically and to be delivered from those tormenting feelings of lesbianism. Instantly, I was delivered emotionally. Thank God, he delivered me before I could have a lesbian encounter! But my physical problems lingered. I was not disappointed however; I simply believed. Somehow, Pastor Emerson's preaching had been enough to get me started on the road to recovery.

Shortly thereafter, I received the baptism of the Holy Spirit with the evidence of speaking in tongues. I stopped looking to the medication to stop me from having seizures. Instead, I began to consistently believe the Word concerning my body regardless of circumstances or the doctor's report. And it worked! Within one year, I was healed from epilepsy and all the other conditions in my body. For the first time in a long time, I was completely free of pain. At this writing, I have gone over twenty years without having a seizure—and this without any assistance from pain pills or medication. I was totally healed by the power of God's Word alone! Praise the Lord!

I knew finally that God had a purpose for me in joining this church where the Word of God came alive in my spirit for the first time ever. I was consistently experiencing God as a deliverer of spirit, soul and body. Due to all these things happening in my life so quickly, I became a faithful member in that church, working where they needed help and wanting just to thank God for everything he was doing for me.

When the next year rolled around, I had a feeling of a different kind. I began to feel that I was to be married soon. This feeling wasn't foreign to me at all because I knew that someday I would get married. And I certainly wanted to get married. However, at this time in my life, I was beginning to wonder if I was every going to be married. I didn't feel this way because I was an old maid, as I was barely 21, but rather because God had given me some instructions that I interpreted as being the death knell of any hope I ever had of experiencing holy matrimony. Allow me to explain.

As stated previously, I became interested in boys at an early age. By the time I was a seasoned teenager, I was full swing into the dating game. I was also very materialistic. I liked and desired things, and I was always trying to get my boyfriends to buy things for me. But I soon discovered that boys don't buy things for girls without expecting something in return.

And what they expected I was not at all willing to give. Now I might not have been the holiest Christian in the world, but I was absolutely hell-scared. When my Baptist pastor preached about premarital sex, he left the impression that it was an unpardonable sin punishable by damnation to hell. Now I didn't know a lot during this time in my life, but one thing I was sure of: I wasn't going to hell, at least not deliberately. So premarital sex was definitely out of the question!

But I still had this desire to have things. And so I became extremely manipulative. It was almost a talent with me. I know now that it was really a demonic empowerment. I learned how to manipulate guys into buying me just about anything I wanted with no sexual favors from me. I learned how to look my seductive best. I paid particular attention to my clothes, hair and nails. My clothes were decidedly form-fitting, outlining enough of my body to titillate any man's sexual appetite. Baby, I knew I had it going on. I was on a mission: I was going to get what I wanted from him without giving him what he wanted from me.

And so with my form-fitting clothes, my seductive ways and my way with words, I was able to reach my objective. I made him think I would deliver, but once I got the goods, I reneged on any promise of sex. You understand, of course, that my promises were usually not communicated verbally but just in the way I conducted myself. Nevertheless, he sincerely thought he would be getting sex. I kept putting him off until the right time, which in my mind, would never come. When it finally became clear that he was growing increasingly impatient, I simply broke off the relationship. I realized later that what I was doing was extremely dangerous. It was only the grace of God that kept me from being hurt or raped. Somebody somewhere was praying for me!

I also had another serious problem. Because I was able to weave in and out of relationships with my virginity still intact and material goods to boot, I became extremely conceited. I boasted continuously about myself. I was proud of the way I looked: my clothes, my hair and my nails. I boasted about all my imagined abilities. The one thing that I was most proud of was my ability to use guys without myself being used by them. (At least I thought that they weren't using me). Anyway, I thought I was the greatest thing on two legs, and I wasn't shy about letting other people know it. I was completely self-absorbed. In short, I really became unbearable. Even my own mother, for a time, couldn't stand me.

Well, I was a Christian at the time, and it didn't take God long to become fed up with what I was doing. One day, he had a little talk with me. He told me that he would not permit me to continue using guys the way I did. To help me comply with His will, He gave me a few instructions. He wanted me to stop making myself so appealing to the opposite sex. I had to lose the form-fitting clothes and the seductive lifestyle.

Initially, I balked at God's instructions. What he was asking me to do made absolutely no sense to me at all. How could I ever attract anyone into my life if I could do nothing to appeal to him physically? I suspected that God wasn't too clued in to this dating thing. I understood of course that according to Proverbs 18:22, it is the man that finds the wife, and not the woman that finds the husband. But I secretly wondered what a man would do with me when he found me looking so plain and unattractive.

But in the end, I concluded that obedience to God was more important than my desire to have a husband. I knew also that God was not going to bless me with Mr. Right as long as there was a chance of me mistreating him the way I did other guys. So I obeyed God, feeling that my fate of being an old maid was forever sealed.

I feel that I must here say that God's dealings with me at this time were unique to me. He was not making a commentary about make-up and clothes. He was not endorsing a doctrine of women not being able to wear make-up and clothes that fit. There is absolutely nothing wrong with a woman looking her absolute best: fake nails, fake hair and all. But there was something wrong with me and my arrogance and manipulative attitude concerning my appearance. God was dealing with me—Kimberly! I knew this, and I never tried to present it as dogma for all Christian young ladies. I never even tried to explain what I was going through. I just obeyed God.

I must admit, however, that I was not prepared for the reaction of other people to my new look. Women especially were disapproving. Not many of the young girls expressed their discontent. I figured they might have been relieved that I was not much competition for them where dating was concerned. They all looked their very best, and there was a general consensus that they would all be married before Sister Kim (as I was affectionately called).

The older women, however, were much more outspoken. They simply failed to understand why someone as young as I insisted on looking so plain. When I tried telling them what God had said to me, they flatly informed me that God couldn't have said those things to me. They told me in no uncertain terms that if I ever wanted to get a man, I would have to do something about the way I looked. I must confess that I believed them, but I had to obey God.

God did vindicate me, however. There were a number of very beautiful, eligible and godly women that attended our church. God could have spoken to Robert about any one of them. But he spoke to him about me. And all of a sudden, the plain Jane was scheduled to marry one of the church's most eligible bachelors. I really believed that he was the best God had to offer. And when my father escorted me down the aisle complete with make-up and a form-fitting wedding dress, I was glad that I had obeyed God.

Remember the feeling I spoke about earlier? You know: the feeling that it was time for me to be married? Well when that feeling came, I didn't know whom I was supposed to marry. I thought it was the guy I was dating, but thank God it wasn't. But the feeling wouldn't go away; so I severed my relationship with one guy and started dating another one, thinking that perhaps he might be the one. But he wasn't either. Both men proposed, but they were simply not God's choice for me.

Now I know you might be thinking: "But Kimberly, how do you know they were not for you?" Well let me tell you a secret that I like sharing with single women. I always prayed and asked the Lord to show me the man before I accepted his proposal. I had a long list of qualifications I wanted in a husband, and these guys did not even meet the first two. At the conclusion of one of these relationships, I was told that only Jesus could meet my expectations. Well, I figured somebody like Jesus would do me good. Nevertheless, I knew that God had someone for me, and I was determined not to settle for less. I honestly believe that my prayer to God along with knowing what I wanted in a husband has made all the difference in my married life.

One day as I was praying, I heard God say these words to me: "The one I have for you is around the corner." With my deep Pentecostal thinking, I figured that God meant that I would be married in a year or so. But come to find out, he meant literally around the corner. You see, my church was around the corner from my house, and that is where I met Robert.

Then during the last week of September '89, an evangelist came to our church to hold a revival. That Friday night of the revival, she challenged all the single women to jump up and praise God if they believed God wanted them to have a good, saved and Holy Spirit filled husband. "A husband," she continued, "who will love you the way the Lord loves you." So I, along with thirty or more single women, shot up out of my seat and started thanking and praising God for a husband. But in the midst of praising God, I heard these words: "Robert is to be your husband."

Now you might be thinking that I really went wild with joy, but I did not. There were two things wrong. First, I didn't know if I was really hearing from God or merely caught up in the excitement of the service. And secondly, I didn't like Robert. Now I know that some of you are probably saying that it was because of his past life of homosexuality. Let me assure you as much as possible that Robert's past had no bearing on my attitude towards him.

In fact, if you can believe this, I did not know that Robert had ever been homosexual. Even though he walked, talked and acted like a homosexual person, I did not see it. Actually, everyone else in the church, including the pastor, knew this about Robert. I now believe that God did not allow me to see that part of him because I am sure that this did one thing would have deterred me in my decision to obey God and eventually take Robert as my husband. It would have at least been an overwhelming obstacle! But still, even though I liked Robert's commitment to the things of God, he was just not my type. Or so I thought.

Now where were we? Oh yes, after hearing those words, I dismissed them. I mean I forgot them, as if they were never spoken. After church, Robert, two other young men and I were standing around talking about how good the service was. After a while, I left them and went to the church office. That's when Robert approached me and asked if I would like to go out to the zoo and maybe a picnic. I agreed to go not because of what God had spoken—remember, I forgot—but out of kindness. He was new to the church, and I felt that perhaps, I could help make him feel at home. I don't know why I thought going to the zoo with him would help him feel more at home. But I did.

I went home that night and told my mother that a guy named Robert who was in the Army wanted to take me out to the zoo and for a picnic. My mother wanted to know who in the world takes a woman to the zoo for a date. I simply replied, "That's where he wants to take me."

Over two weeks would pass, however, before Robert and I were finally able to get together. We had conflicting schedules, and frankly, in the interim, I had simply forgotten about our planned date. Finally, we decided to go out on Columbus Day.

That morning, I went to the post and picked up Robert because at the time, he didn't have a car. In fact, he didn't even know how to drive. We went to the zoo and walked around, looking at the animals and talking about family and church. But Robert kept talking about this girl whom he alleged God had chosen to be his wife. He talked about how pretty she was and how he thought she had a nice personality. He described this girl all the way from the top of her head to the soles of her feet, inside and out, and he wouldn't stop.

Now you might think you could guess what I'm thinking, "Oh yes, I know he's talking about me: how lucky I am." But that was far from what I was thinking. This is what I thought, "I'm out with this guy as a favor and all he can talk about is some girl." I was getting more upset by the minute.

Well, after the zoo, we went out to eat because we hadn't been able to get the picnic items beforehand. Robert started talking about this girl again. I kept trying to change the subject because I was growing increasingly impatient with his ramblings about this girl. Actually, I was getting jealous of a girl I didn't even know.

Now, I know by now, you might be saying to yourself, "Girlfriend, get a clue; if he's out with you talking about a girl, then the girl must be you." Now you get a clue because you know that is not necessarily true! Besides, I wasn't that sharp. Really, I wasn't looking for anyone to date. I would have been content with just being friends with Robert. However, I still considered it rude that he would actually talk about another woman while on a date with me.

After dinner, we decided to go skating. On the drive to the skating rink, lo and behold, the man brought the girl back into the conversation. I remained quiet as he talked about how she was the only one for him. But it soon became difficult for me to continue to hold my peace. At that point, I was steaming on the inside, and my blood pressure hit the top. I got ready to turn to him and really let him have it. Oh I knew of a few words I could say to him: "Why don't you shut up and quit talking to me about this girl. Just go to her; how dare you sit in my car and talk to me about another woman." But before that happened, I heard the Holy Spirit say—more loudly than I have ever heard him—"SHUT UP!" And so I did.

After skating, I dropped Robert off at the base. When we got to his place, he inquired about my plans for the evening. I told him about an Altar Worker's meeting at the church. He wanted to go and even though I didn't want him to, I thought certainly I could not refuse someone the opportunity to attend church. So I told him that I would pick him up at 6:30. When I returned from changing clothes to pick him up that evening, he wanted to know if I had enjoyed our outing. I answered in the affirmative but not truthfully.

We arrived at the church and walked in together, everyone looking at us as if we were a couple. But I had this *we are not together-I'm just giving him a ride* look on my face. After the meeting was adjourned, we walked to the door and began a friendly conversation with an evangelist at our church. She wanted to know how old Robert was. When he said that he was 25, she replied: "Don't you think it is about time for you to settle down and get married?"

Precisely at that moment, I saw what seemed like a big screen television in front of my eyes with someone pushing the rewind button on a VCR. God brought back to my remembrance those words I had heard on that fateful Friday night. And he confirmed that it was indeed He who had spoken them. I, of course, screamed in delightful surprise. And Robert was joyfully relieved that I finally understood that I was actually the girl he had been talking about all day. The evangelist was bewildered at our emotional outburst, but we were able to explain things to her.

As we drove back to the Army post, I kept happily thinking, *I can't believe this whole time he was talking about me, especially considering all the wonderful things he had said.* At the post, we sat in the car for a while and went over the day. We decided that we would date with marriage as our goal. So actually, on our very first date, we decided to get married. Now that was either God or sheer stupidity. But since it has been over twenty years since our first date, and we are still happily together, I am inclined to believe that it was God. We exchanged phone numbers and went our separate ways.

Driving home, I was still in a state of shock. I couldn't wait to get home and tell my mother about what had happened. I soon arrived home and parked my car. When I walked inside, my mother inquired about my day. I told her the whole story from the beginning to the end. I also included how Robert and I planned to be married the following year. Of course, she thought I had flipped out of my mind. She wondered how I could decide to marry him after just one date.

I couldn't blame her, however. I really didn't have a good track record when it came to things like this. She still remembered the other two boyfriends (before Robert) whom I had been sure I would marry. Could I be making yet another mistake? I told her that God himself had informed me that Robert was to be my husband more than two weeks ago. She was still unconvinced. She simply retorted, "Uh, huh, we'll see." But I was undaunted. I went to bed thinking about how God can speak to a woman and tell her whom to marry if she would only ask Him, and then prepare herself to listen and accept what He has to say.

Chapter Two

THE BIG REVELATION
from her perspective

In Psalms 37:4, God gives us a promise that I still hold dear to my heart. He tells us to:

> **"Delight thyself also in the Lord, and He shall give thee the desires of your heart."**

When you look up the word *desire* in the dictionary, you will find that it means "a wanting or longing; strong wish or a wish expressed in words; request." However, most people would probably say that the chances of receiving exactly what you ask of God are slim to none. Fortunately, that was not my thinking at the time. As a child, I had always heard my mother say that I could eventually have whatever I ask from God. My church also confirmed my mother's words with regular teachings on the eagerness of God to answer the prayers of his children.

Because of this teaching in my church, I should have known that God would give me exactly what I asked for in a husband. But the simple fact is that the devil was not willing to let me marry Robert without a fight. And so even though I knew and believed that God had said that Robert was to be my husband, I let doubt slip in as to whether or not he was exactly all that I had asked God for.

There was one thing about Robert that I absolutely had to get settled in my mind. He had to be a virgin. Yes! A virgin! The dictionary defines a virgin as "a [person] who has never had sexual intercourse." Another definition implies someone who is pure and spotless. Before I go any further, let me satisfy your curiosity: yes, I was a virgin! And being a virgin was something that I was at last not ashamed of. Now you may be quick to say that no one is pure. And I may agree with you to a point. However, at the time, my personal definition of someone being pure and spotless was someone that had never dated or even kissed another woman.

Well you may be thinking, *now Kimberly what made you think that God would do that for you?* My answer to that question is found in Matthew 7:7, "Ask and it shall be given." Because of my upbringing, I have always believed that God wants to give His children what they ask for. You may also be wondering how I arrived at such a request. Well, we must take a little side journey so that I can explain it.

While I was dating, my boyfriends would constantly compare me with their former girlfriends. Naturally, this made me really upset. They seemed to get a kick out of determining who the better kisser was: their former girlfriends or I? They would compare my hair, nails, shoes and clothes and even the shape of body. As a woman, the one thing I hate, and probably other women can agree, is being compared with other women.

So right then, I made a decision early in life to marry a virgin. That way, he would have no experiences with which to compare me. Not only did I ask God for a virgin, but I also proceeded to define to God exactly what I thought a virgin was. As I recall, my exact words to God were, "I want a man who has never even touched a woman." When I mentioned this to one of my friends, she jokingly commented that I wanted to marry a priest. To which I abruptly replied, "Well, if that's what it takes, so be it." It still sometimes amazes me that God answered my prayer to the tee, and it didn't take a priest.

Now back to the story at hand. I knew that Robert would be calling me that night after he finished his classes for the evening. I determined that I would get my question answered when he called. When the phone rang, I ran quickly to answer it. Just as I expected, it was Robert.

We started off just talking about our day and other things that make absolutely no sense except to people in love. Then I told him that I had a question that I was finding difficult to ask. Robert quickly assured me that I could ask him anything. That was good enough for me. So, I asked him, "Have you ever had sex before?"

His reply was not exactly what I was fishing for, "If you mean am I a virgin, then no, I am not."

There were a few seconds of silence as my heart dropped inside me with disappointment. Robert must have sensed something was wrong because he quickly said, "I've been meaning to talk with you about that."

I said determinedly, "Let's talk about it now!"

Robert declined sternly, "I need to talk with you face to face." With a date to meet tomorrow at his job, we said our goodbyes until the next evening.

The Bible says in Psalms 91:11 that "[God] shall give his angels charge over you to keep you in all your ways." I did not know what that verse meant at the time, but I was about to experience a real-life application. After getting off work that evening, I couldn't wait to see Robert. I raced home, changed clothes rather quickly, jumped into the car and off I went. I was driven more by a sense of curiosity than a desire to see Robert.

When I arrived at the Army post, Robert was waiting for me outside. He got into the car and as was our usual custom, we went to get something to eat. After dinner, we returned to the post. After parking the car, I looked at Robert, fully expecting an explanation of the statement he had made the previous evening. Robert took a deep breath and began telling me about his past. He informed me how he used to be a homosexual as well as how he got into the lifestyle of homosexuality.

He continued to explain to me about the many different encounters he'd had with other guys. He did not hide one thing. He even told me how long it had been since his last encounter as well as when he had been totally delivered from homosexuality, even down to the very day. Robert also told me many other personal things involving homosexuality. I learned later that Robert told me some things that evening that he had never before, nor have since, shared another human being.

Perhaps at this time, you may think that you could probably guess what I was thinking. But quite possibly, you would be absolutely wrong. You might not believe what I am about to tell you, and frankly I wouldn't either if I had not experienced it. While Robert was talking, my mind seemed as blank as a black sheet of paper. It seemed that no thoughts came into my mind, and no thoughts went out.

Later, I summed up the experience like this: on that night God himself gave charge to his angels to surround my car and to make sure that no demon in hell could get anywhere close to it. I believe He had angels posted inside the car, above it and under it. I believe that his angels covered every opening. I believe this because I am a woman. And I know that means that sometimes my mind can simultaneously process information, think on things, form opinions and virtually never shut up. But on that night, there was simply a blank screen.

After about an hour of baring his soul, Robert looked at me and said, "Now you know why I answered no to your question. And why I insisted that we talk in person. I didn't want to tell you something like this over the phone."

Then he wanted to know if I had anything to say. At that moment, only one thought entered my mind: *past is past*. I verbalized this thought to Robert. He seemed to breathe more easily. He also told me that at any time I had questions about his involvement in homosexuality, I should feel free to ask them of him. In the meantime, I was surprised at how calmly I was handling Robert's revelation of his past.

Still, there was the matter of this "virgin" thing. Robert didn't consider himself a virgin because he had participated in homosexuality though he had not so much as even looked longingly at another woman. I was of a different opinion, however. I believed that according to the Bible, genuine sex could only be between a man and a woman. I did not believe that participation in homosexual activity was reason enough for Robert to think that he was not a virgin. As far as I was concerned, he was a virgin. He thought about it for a moment and then quickly agreed with my line of reasoning.

You may or may not agree with me. However, the bottom line is, virgin or not, Robert was exactly what I had asked God for: a man who had never even touched a woman. The irony doesn't escape me though. I would never have guessed that God would completely deliver a homosexual in order to fill the bill. Nevertheless, I was greatly relieved to finally realize that God had answered my prayer concerning what I desired in a husband. *Thank you, Jesus!* We uttered our fond farewells, as I started for home.

I parked the car in front of my home and went inside. All was quiet as everyone had retired for the evening. I went to my room. Suddenly, it seemed that I smashed right into Satan. He said, "Count how many months it's been since his last encounter. And count the time since he has actually been delivered."

Foolishly, I obeyed and counted six months all together. Then suddenly, a spirit of fear grabbed me. I became scared, nervous and confused all at the same time. Satan continued to tell me that I was going to die from AIDS, and if we had children, they would die as well. That night, I couldn't sleep because my mind was so consumed with thoughts about AIDS. I wondered if Robert had it. I wanted to know when he was last tested or if he had ever been tested. Could I get it from kissing him? All kinds of strange questions assaulted my mind. Fortunately, the Holy Spirit reminded me that Robert had established an open door policy, saying that I could talk to him about anything and at any time. I was confident that he would tell me the truth. So I decided to speak with him tomorrow. And with that, I fell into a restful sleep.

Chapter Three

FREE INDEED
from her perspective

I was becoming more and more dependent on the Word of God. One passage that became particularly helpful to me can be found in Isaiah 54:17:

> **"No weapon that is formed against thee shall prosper; and every tongue that shall rise up against thee in judgment thou shalt condemn."**

That next day I awakened and impatiently waited for Robert to call. I was eager to ask him all my questions. He eventually called and asked if I wanted to get together. Without the least bit of hesitation, I told him that I'd meet him in 15 minutes. We went out for dinner and talked about our day. Towards the end of our evening together, I finally summoned enough courage to pose the question of whether or not he had been tested for AIDS. He assured me that not only had he been tested but that he had also received negative test results. He even provided me with proof of the test results, which he had recently received in the mail. As it turned out, the Army tested twice a year. Robert assured me that he would be happy to share those results with me, as they became available. He didn't want me to worry. And I took some measure of comfort in that fact.

On December 7, 1989, Robert confirmed our commitment to marry by presenting me with an engagement ring. We had dinner that evening at Red Lobster and then drove back to the post. Robert indicated that he had something to tell me. Even though we had decided to get married from the onset of our relationship, I had no idea that Robert had chosen this day to formally propose to me. And so I was greatly surprised when he opened the black velvet box that contained my ring. I was equally surprised when he popped the proverbial question, *Will you marry me?* Of course, you know how I answered him. Because of that night, Red Lobster has become one of my favorite restaurants. I don't even care much for seafood, but Red Lobster still has sentimental value for me.

However, Robert's proposal brought me face to face with something that I had only casually faced before now. With my acceptance of the ring, I had cemented our plans for marriage. In other words, my union with Robert—and all that he was or was not—was fast becoming a reality. I had to finally face and deal with the reality that I had pledged, and that God had instructed me, to live the rest of my life with someone that had once been a homosexual. No longer could I hide behind a religious mask of feigned indifference. The fears that had merely played at the back of my mind had now surfaced full-fledge at the center of my attention.

Consequently, the next four months of our dating tenure can be summed up in a couple of words: PURE HELL! This, of course, was not because of anything Robert did. In fact, Robert perhaps more than any other person, was primarily responsible for helping me get through this period in my life. The devil was the culprit. He was constantly bringing all kinds of thoughts to my mind. I was being tormented day and night. The devil used every available medium in his attacks against me. It seemed that everything I saw on television had something to do with AIDS. The literature that came across my path abounded with reports of AIDS. Every person I talked with brought up the subject. Even my mother was talking about it.

During this time, I watched a movie on television that seemed innocent at the onset. As the story unfolded, however, it was about an ex-homosexual man that married the girl of his dreams. The blushing bride, of course, was oblivious of his past history of homosexuality. As a couple, they seemed the epitome of happiness until one day he became sick. To the shock and dismay of his wife, it was revealed that her husband had full-blown AIDS.

As the story unraveled, he eventually died from AIDS. She also tested positive. She was devastated as she faced what would soon be a life filled with agony, pain and eventual death. What's more, all her friends had warned her against marrying this guy. This part of the movie especially rang true with me because I had one friend in particular that repeatedly voiced concern about my impending marriage to Robert. By the end of the movie, Satan had succeeded in providing yet another vivid image of what he wanted me to believe would happen to me. I could not ignore the striking similarity of the movie to my own situation. Was it possible that I was making the same mistake?

You can guess that with this all going on month after month, I became a nervous wreck. I had talked with Robert plenty of times—more like every time—about my feelings and how the devil had been badgering me. And he answered my every question, sometimes over and over again. This is one of the qualities that I still love about him. No matter how many times I asked, he answered untiringly. He never expressed impatience or offense at my constant interrogation. In fact, many times Robert would pray for me because he understood that in order for us to have a successful marriage, I would have to learn how to deal with his past.

Apart from being able to talk with Robert, I had very little success speaking with other people. This was very difficult for me because in the past, I had always depended on the counsel of other people. There were two people whose solid advice had always been helpful to me: my mother and an older friend who functioned as a big sister to me. I immediately eliminated my mother as a possible confidante because I knew that she could not give me an objective opinion.

I was, however, able to speak with my friend who was able to guess, by Robert's mannerisms, that he was either currently involved or had once been involved with homosexuality. She was not at all shy about offering her assessment of my situation. To her, it seemed a no-brainer. From where she stood, Robert was too big a risk. She reiterated all the fears that the devil had planted in my mind. As a registered nurse, she cautioned me about the possibility of AIDS in my future. She instructed me to wait at least five years before marrying Robert. Though I understood and appreciated her concern, I wondered if her advice was God's final word on the matter.

The funny thing was that when I informed Robert of her suggestion, he immediately said he was willing to wait more than five years if necessary. He was not even offended by her suggestion or doubts about his deliverance from homosexuality. The Bible says that a man who finds a wife finds a good thing. Robert assured me that a good thing was well worth waiting for.

The fact remained, however, that God had actually instructed me to take Robert as my husband. It just did not make sense to me that he would want me to wait five years to obey him. Besides that, I didn't want to wait! I wanted to deal with and overcome those negative feelings. I didn't want the devil ever dictating how I would respond to God's instructions.

In Galatians 1:15-16, Paul reveals a principle that has proven to be a source of strength to me throughout the years:

"But when it pleased God ... to reveal his Son in me that I might preach him among the heathen; immediately I conferred not with flesh and blood."

In other words, Paul is saying that when he has heard from God, he is not looking to see what others think. Of course, he is not saying that we should never seek the advice of others. In fact, the book of Proverbs informs us that there is safety in the multitude of counselors. So then there comes a time when a person must defer to the wisdom of others. On the other hand, however, when the counsel of others runs against the word that you have clearly heard from the Lord, then you must always go with what God is saying.

The day would finally arrive when I, like Paul, would cast aside the wisdom of others—even though they obviously had my best interests at heart—and cast myself fully on the counsel of God. That was the day that I became fed up with the torment. I was praying and crying out to God to settle permanently two issues that burned in my heart. First, I wondered if Robert would ever get a positive reading for AIDS: ten years from now, even thirty years from now. And secondly, I wanted to know that he was totally delivered from that lifestyle. In other words, *would he ever be returning to homosexuality?*

There were at least two reasons for my intense struggle with doubt. As an employee in the medical field, I had been taught that sometimes it could take up to ten years for a positive result to show up on a test. Additionally, I had known friends that had been delivered from homosexuality revert back into that lifestyle. From that, I knew that building a life free of homosexuality was an extremely difficult undertaking. Besides that, by Robert's own admission, I learned that this was his second attempt to live a life free of homosexuality. How could I know that it would be his last?

So then, I had to hear from God. Otherwise, there was no guarantee that Robert would be safely mine regardless of his obvious, good intentions. It no longer mattered what my mama thought. It didn't matter how my friends felt. In fact, it didn't even matter what Robert said, or that he loved me. I absolutely had to hear from God!

So the concerns that had me on the altar that day had festered in my heart for months. I told God in no uncertain terms that I would not have him toying with my emotions. I was not like some dog going for a piece of meat being dangled before his face and then suddenly snatched from his reach. Perhaps you can't imagine speaking to God this way. But I knew beyond a shadow of a doubt that God was the only one that could give me the peace I so desperately needed. I was more concerned with getting an answer than I was with protocol. In my estimation, I had legitimate issues that needed to be resolved. And I would be put off no longer! About two weeks later, I was reading my Bible and came across this passage of scripture:

> **Ask, and it shall be given you; seek, and ye shall find; knock, and it shall be opened unto you: For everyone that asks receives; and he that seeks finds; and to him that knocks it shall be opened. Or**

> what man is he of you whom if his son asks for bread, will give him a stone? Or if he asks for a fish, will he give him a serpent? If you then being evil know how to give good gifts unto your children, how much more shall your Father which is in heaven give good things to them that ask him (Matthew 7:7-11).

As I read this, God gave me his own personal commentary as it related to my situation:

"Do you think that if you ask for a husband, I would give you someone with the AIDS virus? I only give my best to my children, and I have given my best to you."

Hearing this took care of one of my questions. Now, what about the other one? I know you think that perhaps I should have been satisfied, but if I were to give myself 100% to Robert, then I needed to have all my questions answered. And you know I discovered that my questions were not a problem to God. Besides, I never have to settle. God is big enough to answer all my demands. There is no question on this earth that could ever stump God. I wasn't being disrespectful. I was simply needful and in faith and tenacity, I went to the only One who could completely satisfy my needs.

Later in the week, I was reading another passage of scripture. This one can be found in Acts 10:1-28, and is too lengthy to quote in its entirety here. The gist of it is that God is instructing Peter not to call the Gentiles unclean, especially those he had cleansed. God then reminded me that I had been present when Robert was delivered. I had witnessed his deliverance firsthand. Even though at the time I really did not know Robert, I was sure that day that he had been delivered. Dare I now call him whom God had cleansed unclean?

Suddenly, a peace came over me as if someone had poured it on me. I felt it flow from the top of my head to the soles of my feet. Accompanying that peace was the still small voice of the Holy Spirit, "Robert is clean and will never go back into that lifestyle ever again. You have my word on it." Immediately, I began to shout, leap and rejoice! After four months of sheer torment, I was at last free. At that moment, I did not care what anyone else thought of Robert. He was my man—sealed, stamped and delivered by the Holy Spirit, Himself—and I loved him very much.

As far as I was concerned, God forgave and totally delivered him and set him free from homosexuality. Indeed, past is past. Later that year, I happily gave myself totally, spirit, soul and body to Robert as his wife forever. It has been over twenty years now, and my conviction about Robert's deliverance has not wavered or lessened in the least.

CONCLUSION

HEART TO HEART

Now you know my side of this wonderful and very interesting story. But I could not end it without saying something to someone who may be going through the same thing: either dating or already married to a person that used to be a homosexual. You may still be going through the torment in your mind concerning that person's past and would like to walk in the same freedom and deliverance that I've experienced throughout the years. The first thing you need to do is follow 1 Peter 5:7:

"Casting all your cares upon him; for he careth for you."

Jesus wants you and me both to remember that He has our best interest at heart. He knows that worry is the open door for Satan to come into your life to steal, kill and destroy (see John 10:10). And the last thing God wants is for that to happen to you. Let me rephrase that. It's not the last thing God wants for you, but rather it is the thing that he NEVER wants to happen to you!

And the Bible admonishes us in II Corinthians 2:11 to not be ignorant of the devil's devices. We must constantly remember that God has given us His Word, and the Name and the Blood of Jesus to defeat Satan in every attack. If we expect to be victorious at all over the skillfully placed darts of the enemy against our lives, then we must determine to use the weapons of our warfare against him. We can never afford to stay silent when the devil comes around with his tormenting thoughts.

Again in I John 4:4, the Bible emphatically states, "Greater is He that is in you, than he that is in the world." No attack Satan can bring to your mind or body is greater than God's delivering power. God was the one that created Lucifer before he fell into pride and you can be sure that God can handle him, even now when it seems that the devil is pressing in to destroy your very sanity.

Please understand that everything that God gives us is good and perfect, and even if it seems imperfect from a natural standpoint, God has a way of changing things. We must never judge people from the outside or from what they used to be. We should always remember that we were not perfect when Jesus Christ came to live in our hearts. Has He not changed you? Are you not different, though still progressing, from when you first began your Christian journey? Then why do you find it difficult to believe in the transforming power of God for other people?

The Word of God says that man looks on the outside, but God looks on the inside. And so must we. If God has truly spoken to your heart and put you together with that man or woman, then what man or devil can separate you? Don't look to other people so much for wisdom and guidance, but look to the wisdom that is in the Word of God and in his gentle leading by the Holy Spirit. Again, seeking and yielding to the counsel of others is Biblical. And you certainly need to seek counsel when necessary. Particularly if you find yourself suddenly, and without warning, dealing with a revelation of homosexuality regarding your spouse, it is highly likely that you will need godly counseling. Just do not—I repeat, do not—leave God out of your search for wisdom and help.

Let me also say this: the Bible cautions us to be as wise as serpents. In other words, before you trust yourself with anyone the way I did with Robert, be sure you are hearing from God. You don't have to be in a hurry. It took me several months to resolve the issues I had with Robert. He was very patient with me, willing to wait years if necessary. You need to take the time to process through your feelings, your questions and your concerns. Just don't do it without God. With Robert, there was absolutely no pressure. So if you are dealing with someone who is pressuring you, that person is likely not the mate God has for you. At the very least, he or she needs to achieve a level of spiritual maturity before you commit to the relationship. I am glad that I took the time to really hear from God concerning Robert. It has made all the difference in the world in our marriage!

At this writing, it has been over twenty years since the day that Robert came into my life, and I have NEVER once regretted it or wished for anything different. With Robert, I have experienced that God is faithful to keep His word and bring it to pass, no matter what. Remember also that God is a deliverer of spirit, soul and body, even if that person used to me a homosexual. Remember also no matter what: ***PAST IS PAST***.

Would you like to be set free now from torment concerning your mate's past? It doesn't matter if your mate used to be a homosexual, an alcoholic, a drug user, an adulterer or whatever. If so, please pray this prayer out loud and believe that God will deliver you at this very moment.

"Father God, I come to you in the Name of Jesus as my deliverer, and I ask that you will totally deliver me from my spouse's past. And deliver me also from all the torment that the devil is putting me through. I now cast all my cares and worries over on you and ask that you would bring healing into my spirit, soul and body concerning my mate's past.

Now Satan I bind and rebuke you in the Name of Jesus. I take authority over you and command you to leave me alone in Jesus' Name. You will no longer torment me. God has not given me the spirit of fear and torment but of power, love and a sound mind. Therefore, I submit myself to His Word and command you to flee.

Now Father, I thank you that I am free from Satan's power over my mind. And now, I am free to be a witness to others concerning your delivering power. In Jesus' Name, AMEN"

Now go about your way rejoicing. Rejoice regardless of how you feel. Rejoice regardless of what the devil may say. For if you prayed that prayer, Jesus Himself has set you free. And whom the Son has set free is free indeed.

Questions and Answers

The purpose of this section is to provide some answers that I believe are crucial to maintaining a life free of homosexuality. These are questions that may have come up during the reading of this book that perhaps were not answered satisfactorily in the context of the book. This section (as well as the entire book) is for everyone: those of you who are currently involved in homosexuality, those who have been delivered from homosexuality, and even those who are relatives of people who are now or have been involved in homosexuality. And the way to be delivered, and maintain deliverance, from homosexuality is the way to be delivered from any sin. Therefore, this chapter is for anyone caught in any type of bondage, and unfortunately, that is almost everyone.

1. **Am I born this way?**

When it comes to homosexuality, this is perhaps the question of the hour. And science and secular society are doing all they can to answer the question in the affirmative. The idea, it seems, is that if homosexuality can be proven to be a predetermined consequence of birth, then it can be deemed normal and acceptable behavior. If this is the case, then those struggling with feelings of homosexuality can embrace those feelings without fear of moral repercussion.

For years, I struggled with this issue myself especially at times when it seemed that I would never be free of homosexuality. In fact, I was often advised that my aspirations to be heterosexual would die unfulfilled because I was simply not wired that way. Try as I did to heed such advice, I was never able to gain any measure of comfort with homosexuality. I finally had to realize that no scientific discovery of any magnitude could ever silence the voice of my conscience. As desperately as I wanted homosexuality to be right, I could not escape the fact that everything within me screamed in unison that it was wrong. In the end, I had only two alternatives: cease from homosexuality or be doomed to a life plagued with internal unrest. And if you have experienced internal strife at all, then you understand why I made the choice to give up homosexuality.

Even in the years since my deliverance from homosexuality, this question has many times crossed my mind. For those of you, especially Christians, who have never been involved with homosexuality, this question is perhaps a no-brainer. But I've lived this life! I know what it's like to be overwhelmed by feelings so strong that they indeed seem to be a natural part of you, especially when you've had those feelings since childhood. Actually, it is much easier to concede to homosexuality as a consequence of birth than to wrestle against such irresistible feelings. For this reason, I honestly believe that the vast majority of homosexuals are sincere in their belief that they were meant to be this way. So then, the question is one that has to be dealt with.

Frankly, I don't know a lot about science. And it is beyond me to imagine that the entire scientific community has conspired to manufacture information in order to justify homosexuality. (I didn't say that it couldn't possibly happen; I just can't imagine it). But perhaps, there is a gene that is predisposed towards homosexuality. I honestly do not know. What I do know absolutely is that homosexuality is wrong—gene or not! And what I am trying to get across to you is that it does not matter how you were born. You can change! If you believe that you were born with homosexual tendencies, I will not try to convince you otherwise. However, there is something you must know: you can be born again!

One of the things I realized early in life is that it would be unjust of God (and God is not unjust) to condemn a behavior without providing a way of escape. Homosexuality is wrong, but God has made a way out of it. By placing faith in Jesus Christ, you could not only put an end to homosexuality, but you could also acquire a brand new life. However, this is a decision you only can make. Apart from scientific evidence. Apart from the advice of your friends. Even apart from your own very real feelings and desires.

2. **How do I stop?**

I have often heard people say that it is impossible to be free from homosexuality. No doubt, you are aware of the old adage: "Once a thief..." But thank God, I know that's not true! If you genuinely want to be free, then you can be free. However, the very first thing you must do is agree with God that homosexuality is wrong! Forget what society thinks. Forget how you feel. Consider what God has to say about homosexuality.

> **And likewise also the man, leaving the natural use of the woman, burned in their lust one toward another; men with men working that which is unseemly, and receiving in themselves that recompense of their error which is meet (Romans 1:27)**

From this passage of scripture, we can deduce a number of things about homosexuality. First, it is NOT normal or natural. This may sound bigoted to you, but the natural expression of sex is heterosexuality, and that within the context of marriage. Secondly, according to this scripture, homosexuality is unseemly. I ran a cross reference on the word *unseemly* with a computerized thesaurus and came up with the following synonyms: *indecent, improper, unbefitting,* and *inappropriate*. And check this one out: *wrong*. That's right:

homosexuality is just plain wrong! Also from this passage of scripture, we can deduce that there is a recompense or punishment for homosexuality.

I know I might be coming across to you as narrow-minded and insensitive to the plight of homosexuals. But remember that I was once homosexual. I understand all too well how difficult it is to sit where you are and listen to what I am saying. However sympathetic I might be to your feelings, I can only tell you the truth. And frankly, telling you the truth does not bother me one bit. Because I also know how marvelous and awesome it is to finally walk free of homosexuality's dogged control. And the only thing that can make you free is the truth that is found in the Bible. So please, I beg you: don't turn me off, but listen to what I am saying. With my whole heart, I am trying to help you.

After you agree with God that homosexuality is a sin, then the biggest part of your battle is over. You now simply need to repent of your sin and accept the lordship of Jesus Christ. You can do this by sincerely praying the following prayer:

> *Lord Jesus, I agree with you that homosexuality is a sin. And for all these years, I have been sinning. But I know now that you love me, and that you are willing and able to help me. I also believe that you are the Son of God who died for my sins and was raised again for me to be right with God. I accept your word of grace and ask you to come into my life and be my Lord and Savior forever. Thank you, Jesus.*

If you prayed that prayer, then you have just become born again. In other words, your old life of homosexuality has just been replaced with a new life in Christ Jesus (see II Corinthians 5:17). You are completely brand new on the inside, and the probability of you living free from homosexuality is 100%! However, you must learn how to let the new life on the inside control your life on the outside. For this reason, you might want to re-read the section in this book that discusses how to stay free from homosexuality. You also need to immediately find a good church that teaches and believes whole-heartedly in the Bible. That way, you'll be able to stay free. Make no mistake: there will be obstacles along the way. But because of your decision to trust Jesus, God is now in covenant with you, and He personally will empower you to surmount every obstacle. Believe me: I know what I'm talking about. It has been many years (over twenty) and even more obstacles than years since my deliverance from homosexuality, but I am still free. And my life just keeps getting better.

3. **There is this guy that goes to my church. He claims to be a Christian who has been delivered from homosexuality. And yet he has such strong feminine mannerisms. Is it possible that he could really be delivered?**

Absolutely! Mannerisms are a deeply ingrained part of the homosexual lifestyle. They often begin very early in life and are developed to the point of becoming a mighty stronghold. For this reason, they rarely disappear at the onset of deliverance from homosexuality. In fact, they can linger for years after a person has actually been set free. Feminine mannerisms especially are hard to get rid of because they have become entrenched as a natural part of homosexual behavior. Often, a person is not even aware that he may be acting in a feminine manner.

One of the biggest mistakes Christians make is that of passing judgment based on external behavior. Perhaps, homosexuality provides the greatest opportunity for Christians to make such a mistake. In other words, Christians especially often mistake feminine mannerisms as indisputable evidence of homosexuality. The irony is that masculine mannerisms in a woman, unless extremely exaggerated, are most likely attributed to tomboyishness or maybe even strength. The fact of the matter is that people hardly ever automatically assume that a masculine woman is a lesbian.

On the other hand, a man that exhibits feminine mannerisms is almost always believed to be homosexual. However, it is possible that he may not have ever been involved in homosexuality at all. Or maybe, and this is highly likely, he is someone that has been delivered from homosexuality but has not yet overcome the mannerisms that are such a large part of homosexuality.

For years, this was my situation exactly. I had been set free from homosexuality and was living in close fellowship with the Lord. And yet, I just could not shake those feminine mannerisms. As a result, people (even other Christians) invariably perceived me to be a homosexual. And of course, many of those people wanted nothing to do with me. This would have been devastating had I not learned to focus on Jesus and his attitude towards me rather than the perception of other people. Consequently, I was able to press to become virtually free from the feminine mannerisms that had been such a big part of my life for so many years. And though there are still some skeptics—I imagine there always will be—I don't get very many people second-guessing my sexual orientation.

The very best thing you can do for people who are newly saved is to refrain from judging them by their physical appearance. Besides the possibility of being dead wrong, you also risk offending and isolating a fellow Christian. If you really must judge, then do it the Bible way and judge them by their fruit. Physical manifestations such as feminine mannerisms can hardly be classified as fruit and so are never to be used as a basis of judgment. Ultimately, the best thing to do is to refrain from judging others as much as possible. Pray for people, speak candidly with them and allow them room to develop, realizing that we are all simply works in progress. But oh, what glorious works we are!

4. **How do I rid myself of feminine mannerisms?**

This is a very important question simply because it is very important for a man to be as free as possible of overtly feminine mannerisms. It took me some time to realize that God wanted to do more than just deliver me from homosexuality; He wanted those mannerisms gone as well. Feminine mannerisms are a particular hindrance in forging friendships, especially with other males. Let's face it: most men are uncomfortable with other men that display overtly feminine mannerisms. Feminine mannerisms might also cast a negative shadow on your Christian witness. It is difficult, though not impossible, for people to believe the testimony of a man that is overtly feminine. I must admit, however, that it has been my experience that most women have no problem accepting such testimony.

Doubtlessly, it is important to abstain from judging people by outside appearances. However, for the person with a past of homosexuality, it is equally important for him to eliminate any behavior that might be conducive to an unjust judgment. In other words, you've got lose those feminine mannerisms!

At one point in my life, this was a difficult issue for me to face. If the truth were told, I really didn't think that I could change. After all, I had harbored feminine mannerisms most of my life and at one time had even tried to extinguish them, but to no avail. Besides that, I was somewhat resentful of all those people that judged me by my mannerisms and consequently doubted that I had really been delivered from homosexuality. It was difficult for me to understand why they could not see what was obvious to me: that I'd had a genuine encounter with God that had impacted my life forever. I had to eventually realize that the problem was not so much the doubters as it was the mannerisms. Deep inside, I knew that I wanted to change, but repeated failed attempts to change rendered it too painful for me to ever try again.

Finally with the help of a very good friend, I was able to admit that my mannerisms were indeed problematic and needed to be eliminated or at least controlled. But you guessed it: that was easier said than done. Following that friend's suggestion, I chose a particularly masculine guy and tried to pattern my mannerisms after his. But that did not work. The person I chose was a television personality whom I didn't particularly care for. Therefore, I found it difficult to consistently mimic his mannerisms. My effort to eradicate my feminine mannerisms was fast becoming a laborious and fruitless undertaking. And so eventually, I simply stopped trying.

At that, the most surprising thing happened. The mannerisms, with very little to no effort from me, began to disappear. As time wore on, I began to become more masculine. Although the process is still ongoing, I believe that I can say without fear of contradiction that my mannerisms are 100% better.

In the meantime, I realized that just as God had delivered me from homosexuality, He was waiting to transform my mannerisms as well. I simply had not allowed him to. When it boils right down to it, everything that God does is a matter of faith. Although I believed everyday that God had freed me from homosexuality, I found it difficult to believe that the same God could free me from those feminine mannerisms. In other words, I limited God with my thinking. And as long as I did this, the feminine mannerisms persisted. When I finally did realize that God wanted me free from the mannerisms as well, I tried to change the mannerisms myself. This only resulted in failure and frustration.

At last, I conceded, I thought, to the mannerisms, but I was actually conceding to God. This allowed the Holy Spirit to move in and lead me to victory over those mannerisms. The Holy Spirit spent a lot of time telling me how to walk, how to talk, how to sit, etc. Many times, in the middle of an activity, I would be confronted by the gentle but correcting voice of the Holy Spirit. For instance, I might be sitting with my legs crossed in a feminine manner. The Holy Spirit would say to me, "Don't sit with your legs crossed like that." Invariably, when the Holy Spirit came to me with instructions, I would submit to them. As such, it became a matter of obedience and a matter certainly easier and more productive than trying to deal with those mannerisms in my own strength.

My advice to you would be not to concentrate so much on your mannerisms but rather on the leading of the Holy Spirit. You can see the importance of being in a good church so that you can learn how to discern the voice of the Holy Spirit. You'll find that your success with anything in life is totally dependent upon how well you recognize the voice of the Holy Spirit. Once you recognize that voice, determine to be obedient to it. You'll soon realize that getting rid of those mannerisms is not so hard after all.

One final word of caution: you absolutely must learn NOT to be so controlled by what people think of you. This particularly means that your motive to change your mannerisms cannot be based on your desire to please other people or even to convince them of the authenticity of your deliverance. I discovered a long time ago that it is far too great an endeavor to try to control what other people think of you. Some people are going to think what they want, no matter what. You simply need to yield to the Holy Spirit, allow him to affect a transformation in your mannerisms and leave other people and their opinions to God.

By the same token, you also cannot hold on to the hurts of your past, especially those hurts that come as a result of someone rejecting, mistreating or prejudging you based on your homosexual orientation. Those of us who have come out of socially condemned lifestyles are sometimes angry at the way we were treated by society. I discovered, however, that in order for me to succeed with God, I had to break down all my walls of defenses constructed as a result of offenses encountered in my past. Simply put, I had to forgive and forget. I had to let go of my past, even the part I wanted to hang on to. Indeed, in order to be completely free from homosexuality, mannerisms and all, you'll have to first be freed from people. It sounds like a lot, but it's all easy to the Holy Spirit. Just follow his leading.

5. How do I deal with the shame of my past?

I don't have to deal with the shame of my past because when God freed me from homosexuality, He also freed me from the shame. The bottom line is that you don't deal with the shame of your past; you get over it. And that goes for anyone, not just people that have been involved with homosexuality. At one point when I tried dealing with the shame of my past, I only became more condemned. The condemnation, in turn, rendered me powerless against the tireless efforts of the devil to regain access to my life. Without the necessary power to resist his attacks, I became once again ensnared by homosexuality.

But God is good! And so he set me free once again. It was at that point that I realized the absolute essentiality of burying my past, shame and all. I don't waste one moment of my time—and it would be a horrible waste indeed!—wrestling with guilt or shame concerning my past. When I say I am free, I mean I AM FREE! I am not filled with shame and condemnation. I am not angry or bitter. I do not suffer with bouts of low self-esteem. I love myself and enjoy being me. I don't even spend any time regretting my past involvement with homosexuality. Simply put, I got over my past years ago. And I absolutely refuse to enter into the worry and condemnation of it ever again!

And I'll let you in on a little secret: the devil doesn't bother me about my past either. Oh, he used to remind me about it quite often. But I finally discovered that his reminders were perfect opportunities for me to offer a sacrifice of praise to God for my freedom from homosexuality. So when he would bring condemning thoughts to my mind, I would invariably respond with loud, grateful praise to God. He finally got a clue and abandoned his efforts to bring me under condemnation about my past. After all, his reminders were doing him more harm than they were me.

This is something that you'll have to do as well. You must decide to not be the least bit bothered by your past. Other people, perhaps even family members, might be bothered, but you don't have to be governed by their feelings. Live with an attitude of gratitude about what God has done for you. Learn to value your freedom to the point that you are willing to guard it at all costs. And then when the devil comes around trying to entrap you again, he'll be no match for you.

I believe that the one thing that really helped me the most was when I realized that God genuinely cares for me. And he has no hang-ups whatsoever about my past involvement with homosexuality. I mean it's hard to be condemned and bothered by my past when God has granted me a full pardon from it. This is a revelation that will do you good as well. Be controlled by what God thinks about you and not by what others think about you. You may not ever again get anyone to accept you. But the only One who really matters—the God and Creator of the entire universe—has already accepted you! You just can't do any better than that! Get ready for a wonderful life. It's great being free!

ROBERT & KIMBERLY
21 Years Later

LOOK AT WHAT THE LORD HAS DONE!

From her perspective

The title of this chapter describes exactly how Robert and I feel about the years since we met. Praise to our Heavenly Father is common in our lives. We can truly look back over our marriage and see the hand of God actively at work. He has truly done many marvelous things on our behalf. Among many things, He has opened doors for us to bring enlightenment to others concerning His freedom in the Name of Jesus. It still overwhelms me how God put Robert and me together. In fact, almost 22 years after our first date, I am still moved to tears of joy and thanksgiving at what the Lord has done. There have been so many things that have happened since we married that it would take another book to share.

In order for a person to continue to inspire the freedom of others, he or she must exhibit consistency. Therefore, I will attempt to give you a brief synopsis of our years of marriage—21 and still counting! This synopsis will make this book more complete as well as reveal the status of our lives since our deliverance. In other words, it will answer the proverbial question: *where are they now?*

Well for starters, Robert is still FREE! I don't mean a little free, but just as free as Jesus is right now in Heaven. Every year I can see and sometimes feel Robert's boldness with sharing his testimony become greater in intensity. Robert is in no way, shape or form ashamed about telling anyone how God set him free from homosexuality. This is a good thing because boldly sharing your testimony plays an important part in walking out your deliverance. When you know that you know that you have been delivered, you will shout it from the housetop and tell everyone you know. Paul writes concerning the gospel in Romans 1:16 (Amp):

For I am not ashamed of the gospel (good news) of Christ, for it is God's power working unto salvation {for deliverance from eternal death} to everyone who believes with a personal trust and a confident surrender and firm reliance, to the Jew first and also the Greek.

Paul was not ashamed to tell others how Christ set him free, forgave him, delivered him and set him on the paths of righteousness. Similarly, Robert is also not ashamed to spread the good news. The Word of God has so much power to set any person free from ANYTHING. All people have to do is share what God has done in their lives, and God will do the rest. God will always back up His Word. Mark 16: 20 confirms, **"they {the disciples or insert your name} went out and preached everywhere, while the Lord kept working with them and confirming the message by attesting signs and miracles that closely accompanied [it]."**

Whenever Robert shares his testimony, I can sense the Anointing on him to minister God's freedom to anyone who is bound by homosexuality. He absolutely loathes the spirit of homosexuality, and even more, he loves the person bound by that spirit. I must confess the devil has tried to test him, but failed BIG TIME. The devil failed because of Robert's commitment to the God of his freedom and his boldness to share his testimony. I'm sure the devil had not counted on Robert witnessing to and praying the prayer of deliverance for the person he used to bring the temptation. A famous television evangelist has said on several occasions that you must embarrass the devil whenever he shows his ugly head. You absolutely must never be nice to the devil, for he means you no good! Robert has done this from day one and continues to do so to this day. After 21 years, I can still report with absolute conviction and confidence that no doubts have ever risen in my mind concerning his deliverance. I simply believed God's word to me that **he would never go back into that lifestyle.**

However, I never imagined then how God would use him to bring the message of victory to so many men, women, boys and girls caught up in this lifestyle. Over the years, we both have had opportunities to minister to parents with children involved in homosexuality. Our hearts go out to them over and over again. When we hear about parents despairing over their very young children who exhibit homosexual tendencies, we cry out to God with them for their children's deliverance. We therefore strive with every fiber of our being to bring this message of deliverance to the whole world. We will continue to do so until Jesus returns.

Let's talk about our children for a moment. Our children know about our past, as we have been straight with them since they were old enough to understand. They have witnessed us share our testimony in private and public settings. They were initially surprised because they could not see it. All they could see was a dad who was strong, godly and masculine, and a mother who exhibited godliness and grace. Our children have come to experience and know that their dad will share his testimony during his sermons, regardless of the audience, if he needs to make a point about God's love and delivering ability. They have heard him share it so much that they can tell it. In fact, our oldest child has shared his testimony several times during ministry sessions with her peers.

This is a good thing because the devil just doesn't quit just because you obtained your deliverance and are going strong. He will always try to get the next generation. The devil looks for any open doors into your children's life. One of the ways you close those doors is to be honest about your past struggles. We have, from the beginning, taught our children how to avoid getting trapped into sin, especially addictive sins, such as sex, alcohol and drugs.

Parents, I must admonish you, especially if you are saved, to do all you can to close any doors you have control over. Don't let your children watch television shows fraught with sex scenes. You shouldn't watch them either. If they are not good for your children, they are not good for you. Besides, you need to be your children's greatest role model. Don't let your teens and preteens frequent places that you know or even suspect will tempt them sexually. Do not be deceived into thinking that the devil cannot get hold of your children. In fact, know that if you don't fight the good fight of faith concerning your children, the devil will prevail against them. Therefore, when you feel an urge in your spirit to pray for your children, DO IT! This is very important because try as you might, you cannot completely shelter them from the world. So you need to have the Holy Spirit working on them at all times. When the Holy Spirit tells you to say something to them, DO IT! Seek help if you need to. The most important thing is that you never stop talking to them, no matter what they say or how they mean-mug you.

Concerning my testimony, I can boldly say that after 22 years, I am still free of seizures, hypoglycemia, arthritis and ulcers, and I am free in my thought life—the most important place to be free! I still have a great passion for wanting people to be free from the bondage the devil brings into their lives. I still enjoy standing and sharing our testimony with some man, woman, boy or girl who is struggling with homosexuality. I want people to walk in freedom. The cry of my heart is for people to be set free from all of the devil's chains. I have been blessed to minister to and pray with a wife who suddenly discovered that her husband had been living a bisexual lifestyle for years. The wife chose to stay, and God not only delivered her husband, but he also healed their marriage. Robert and I both ministered to a couple to help them understand and stand in faith against their daughter's proclivity for lesbianism. I always enjoy showing people, from my personal experience with Robert, that homosexuals can experience deliverance.

I further enjoy helping people realize they don't have to be tormented by thoughts of homosexuality, fornication, adultery or any thoughts from the pit of hell—not one more day! Years ago, God taught me, through 2 Corinthians 10:4-6, how to counter tormenting thoughts: **"Casting down imaginations, and every high thing that exalteth itself against the knowledge of God, and bringing into captivity every thought to the obedience of Christ."** Since then, I have endeavored to show others this same truth and how to live and walk in it. God has done so much for me in my 43 yrs of life and 21 yrs of marriage that I have to tell it. I agree with Paul, **"Woe is unto me, if I preach not the gospel"** (1 Corinthians 6:19). I must preach it, teach it, declare it and share it. There are men, women, boys and girls on the brink of hell and destruction, who need to hear that Jesus came to *heal the brokenhearted, preach deliverance to the captive, and recovering of sight to the blind, to set at liberty them that are bruised, and to preach the acceptable year of the Lord.* Jesus is not interested in anyone being free for one day only, but FOREVER, and I have surrendered my life to being a tool He can use to fulfill this mission. I must do it. I don't want to get any glory; I want my Lord and Savior to be glorified because if He is lifted up, He will draw all people unto Him.

From his perspective

The transformation God has wrought and sustained in me is a powerful and ever-present testimony of His compassion and faithfulness. These days, I hardly recognize the image in my mirror, for it bears absolutely no resemblance to my former self. Romans 12:2 admonishes**, "And be not conformed to this world: but be ye transformed by the renewing of your mind that ye may prove what is that good, and acceptable, and perfect will of God."** Through the years, this is precisely what has happened to me: the Word of God has transformed me so thoroughly that I now bear the perfect will of God—regarding my sexual orientation—in my spirit, soul and body. Even my mannerisms have been transformed!

The awesome thing about transformation is that it reveals the will of God. People all over the world wonder about God: *Is He really good; does He care; can He really make the difference in one's life?* When we cooperate with God to allow His Word to transform us, we become exhibits of God's power and character. In essence, we prove the will of God, that it is good! That is exactly the privilege I've enjoyed in the years since my deliverance. God has used me not only to reveal His will concerning homosexuality but also to reveal His compassion for people and His ability to eradicate the destructive hold of the enemy.

It is the Anointing of Christ Jesus to destroy yokes and remove burdens (Isaiah 10:27). It all happened through the grace of God for which I can take no credit. Of course, I've had to cooperate with God, but it was even the grace of God that enabled that cooperation. And so the Word of God has sustained me. The Word of God has lifted me up and made me stand face-to-face, without cowering, against the enemy of my soul. And the Word of God has caused me to triumph every time.

The incident to which Kimberly refers occurred during a business trip to California. My business finished, I waited in my hotel room that evening until my morning flight back to Georgia. Later in front of the hotel, I strolled the sidewalk, praying in tongues. As I did so, a gentleman approached me and before he could proposition me, I offered him the gospel of the Lord Jesus Christ. During my conversation with him, I learned that he was a married flight attendant, who lived a secret life of homosexuality during flight layovers, away from the watchful eye of his family. I prayed for him, assuring him of God's love, mercy, forgiveness and deliverance.

I can remember when something like this would have sent me running in terror. However, I have come to the place where I understand that the power of God resides in me to positively impact the lives of others. Don't get me wrong: I wholeheartedly adhere to the Biblical injunction to **"make no provision for the flesh."** By the same token, I don't run from a fight, especially when I know that I am well equipped and that the fight could result in someone's deliverance. The fellow I met on the sidewalk that day will never be the same again—all because of the unconditional love of the Father and the Savior He commissioned on behalf of humanity. I tell you: I have never been able to get over the love of God! I've gotten over hurt, shame, disappointment and regret. I've even gotten over the betrayal of friends. But the wooing, compassionate, chastising, wide-armed, Truth-wielding, rescuing, revelatory, soothing, unpretentious, in-your-face, got-your-back love of the Father will always enamor me!

But homosexuality is manifesting itself in an unusual place these days: the Church of the Lord Jesus Christ! I mean *unusual* in its boldness, in its frequency and in its claim. Of course, for years we have suspected, even witnessed, homosexuality in the Church. However, it often operated incognito and confined (usually to the choir stand). The days of down-low Christians seem to be quickly approaching an end. That's not necessarily a bad thing. Keeping homosexuality under wraps simply enabled it to thrive uncontested. In our zeal to keep homosexuality at bay, we hurled condemnations at suspected offenders. We struck angrily every time it reared its ugly head. We thought we were dealing fatal blows, but we simply drove the spirit underground where it somehow gained strength and now fights with a vengeance! Some of us refused to see the proverbial handwriting on the wall; we ignored the growing tide of homosexuality that hiccupped sporadically throughout the Church's development. Alas, we can no longer look the other way. Unpleasant as it may be, it is time—indeed past time—to have a frank, Biblical conversation regarding homosexuality.

The undeniable fact is that homosexuality is in the Church. It is out of hiding, bold and combative. It almost begs for a fight. Its manifestation is frequent! Everywhere you look, somebody in the Church is coming out of the closet—bishops, pastors, renowned musicians, denominational heads and church founders. And people are applauding them! As stated above, homosexuality has long operated in the Church; however, what is different now is its boldness and its claim of Biblical correctness.

Someone questioned me recently about the Church's emphasis on homosexuality, which I considered ironic, because the contemporary Church is lacking in its weigh-in on this particular sin. At any rate, she reasoned that homosexuality is no different from any other sin. In so doing, she unwittingly made my point. Homosexuality requires the Church's attention because there are entire groups of people—within the Church even!—seeking to sanction homosexuality as a godly form of behavior. This makes homosexuality different from say *adultery* or *witchcraft* because for many, it is not even regarded as a sin. In fact, Christians coming out of the closet argue that homosexuality is their God-given orientation. They contend that homosexuality is an unalterable plight of birth. That part of the Church that dares to speak against homosexuality doggedly counters the notion of homosexuality as a consequence of birth.

Divine Design

I empathize with the homosexual-by-birth argument. However, the argument is inappropriate. Because of the fall of humanity, we cannot look to birth as an indication of God's will. Our births are rooted in the fall and are therefore flawed. We must look to divine design for God's will. The divine design for sexual orientation (for anything actually) is found in Genesis. After the creation of man, the Lord God determined that man needed a partner: **"It is** not good for man to be alone; I will make a helper comparable to him" (Gen. 2:18). After considering every beast of the field and every bird of the air, **God "caused a deep sleep to fall upon Adam, and…took one of his ribs [and] made [it] into a woman, and He brought her to the man"** (Gen. 2:21-22). Verse 24 continues, **"Therefore a man shall leave his father and mother and be joined to his wife, and they shall become one flesh."** The commentary in my Bible states that among other things, *one flesh* implies sexual union. Nowhere in this account of creation, which incidentally reveals God's intent for human sexuality, is homosexuality even indicated as part of the divine design. It is clear that God intended man and woman to dwell maritally in sexual union—not man and man or woman and woman. Genesis 1 also contains an account of creation, again with no allusion at all to homosexuality. This lack of allusion is not accidental. It intentionally highlights the divine design for human heterosexuality.

Subsequent Procreation

Had Adam and Eve remained faithful to God's will, a discussion on homosexuality would not be necessary. However, not only did Adam and Eve fall, but they also procreated in their fallen state, hence the principle of subsequent procreation—i.e., procreation following the fall. Incidentally, every human being, after Adam and Eve, was born subsequent to the fall. Genesis 1 reveals that every living thing God created—plants, animals and humanity—contained a seed. It was God's way of perpetuating life without having to literally create each individual. Moreover, each living thing can only procreate after its kind, according to its seed. That means that sinful individuals (that would be everyone as a result of the fall) can only procreate other sinful individuals. No one more than David was aware of the negative issues of subsequent procreation (see the discussion on David and Bathsheba in chapter three). From that discussion, you should understand that how we were born has no bearing on what is right and wrong. Any honest Christian would have to agree that people were born in sin, and since homosexuality is a sin, it is not a stretch to conclude that people can be born with a bent toward homosexuality. This does not mean that homosexuality is right. This simply means that homosexuals were born wrong—that is, from a moral standpoint:

just like me; just like you. This is exactly the reason for the new birth: it cancels the sinful effects of subsequent procreation by transforming its recipient into a new being. II Corinthians 5:17 confirms this truth: **"If anyone be in Christ, he is a new creation; old things have passed away: behold, all things have become new."** The bottom line? Homosexuality is a sinful consequence of birth, which can only be changed through the new birth.

What the Church Must Do: Grace and Truth

The Church must engage! The traditional Church has leaned heavily on the letter of the law when dealing with homosexuality. We've used harsh attitudes and even harsher words to condemn homosexuals. We thought we were helping them, but we only drove them deeper into their closets of shame. And because God often delivers in the open, we have effectively kept many homosexuals from the deliverance they crave. On the other hand, the contemporary Church is so full of so-called grace that it won't even acknowledge homosexuality as a sin. Many contemporary churches won't even broach the subject. On the rare occasion that the contemporary Church addresses homosexuality, it circumvents accountability with platitudes, such *as homosexuality is no greater than any other sin or the Church's job is not to judge*. We must marry grace and truth in order to answer the bold spirit of homosexuality. We must love homosexuals because we cannot effectively minister to people we do not love. Our hearts of contempt must become hearts of compassion. Because the wrath of man does not work the will of God, we must abandon our anger at homosexuals and replace it with genuine, unconditional, longsuffering love. On the other hand, real love always involves truth because we do not really love those from whom we withhold the truth. If we really believe what the Bible says about the penalty of sin, we cannot (in love) remain indifferent. What we must do is commit to always speak the truth and always in love—emphasize **always!**

Alas, this is the clarion call for the Pinkneys. We have been divinely commissioned to spread the message of grace and truth concerning homosexuality. This book is simply one step in the fulfillment of that call. By adhering to the Biblical principles espoused in this book, you are, in effect, helping us to answer the call. And for that, we are immensely grateful!

Acknowledgements

My profoundest thanks!

I believe that no one can complete a project of any worth without influence and assistance from other people. This is perhaps the most enjoyable part of the book for me because this is where I get to express my gratitude to so many people who have meant so much to me in my life! Of course, chief of all those people is my Lord and Savior Jesus Christ, without whose grace and mercy I would not even be alive let alone able to write this book.

My Parents

I am particularly grateful to my parents (Joseph and Mary Pinkney) for bringing me into this world and raising me as best as they knew how. Thank you for all the times you ensured that I was in church whether I wanted to go or not. It was during those early, impressionable years that I formed a love for God and the things of God that the devil has never been able to shake. Thanks especially for teaching me how to work hard. I could not be where I am today without the tireless contribution you both have made to my life.

My Siblings

I am number nine of ten siblings. And within this group, there is a plethora of diverse personalities. My siblings and I have not always seen eye to eye, but I am grateful that they have always treated me very well. For some time now, it has been a mystery to me how they can fuss among each other but rarely fight with me. They have always treated me with dignity and respect. And the most important thing is that they believe in me. It has been my impression that they have always been so proud of me even though I know I didn't always do things just right. Perhaps, they are this way towards me because I am one of the two babies of the family. Whatever the reason, I am eternally grateful for their love and support.

My Other Mama!

Mama Helene is my mother on my wife's side. (We have a solemn agreement not to use the *in-law* word when referring to each other). She has been a tremendous source of support and encouragement not only to me but also to my entire family. She has always treated me with great respect and has been as excited about my dreams and goals as I am. Thank you Mama for accepting me unconditionally into your family as one of your own. I can assure you that my life has been impacted in the greatest possible way since my affiliation with your family.

I will also here like to thank Rev. Darnell Ward. You have always gone beyond the call of duty to make me feel welcome in your family. For this, I am and will always be deeply grateful. I love and appreciate all of you and that does include my siblings on my wife's side!

My Pastors

Chiefly because of my stint in the military, I have had five pastors, all of which have had a strong positive influence on me, all to whom I owe a debt of gratitude.

Pastor **Bradley White** of Atlanta, GA was the first pastor I encountered after my initial deliverance from homosexuality. It was under his ministry that I first discovered that Jesus loves me in spite of my past. His ministry also taught me that I could have a personal relationship with God, that I could talk with him and expect him to talk with me. It was also under his ministry that I received the baptism of the Holy Spirit, which changed my life forever.

When I met Pastor **Leon Emerson** of Denver, CO, I was in a backslidden condition. Because of condemnation, I had allowed the devil to entrap me once again with homosexuality. Pastor Emerson not only prayed for my deliverance from homosexuality, but he also consistently taught me principles that would keep me free. Because of that, I have never again returned to homosexuality. One of the things that struck me about Pastor Emerson and his congregation was that they were not quick to judge me for my past. They simply accepted and loved me, even though they were fully aware of my past. Although I never expressed it, this meant almost as much to me as salvation itself. Additionally, Pastor Emerson and his lovely bride, Yvonne, are supreme examples of what a godly marriage should be. As such, through the years, they have been unwitting marriage mentors to my wife and me.

I met Pastor **Harvey Michael Mueller** during a military tour in Germany. I remember him especially for being the first pastor to personally befriend me. His friendship was particularly endearing because it was unconditional. My past absolutely did not matter to him! In fact, he never once made reference to it. He was only interested in my present relationship with the Lord. Not only did he accept me as a friend and brother, but he also allowed me to preach many times at his church. It was during my tenure with this ministry that I understood clearly that God could still us me regardless of my past. I am grateful to Pastor Mueller for a number of things: his friendship, his patience, his faith in me, his tireless support, etc. But what I am most grateful for is that he helped me to know for certain that I am salvageable to God.

Pastor **John A. Jones** of San Antonio, TX turned out to be one of my best friends of all times. For all the years I was involved in his ministry, he did everything he could to facilitate my growth in the Lord. He also allowed me to minister in his church many times. He was the pastor that seemed to be the most interested in my personal and spiritual development. He would make numerous suggestions about my behavior, attitude, ministry or any area where he felt I needed improvement. I didn't always welcome his advice even though I invariably put it to use. My sojourn with him made me into a mature Christian who is more fitted for the Master's use. For this, Pastor John, I am eternally grateful.

My time under **Pastor Joe Eyler's** ministry was shorter than with the other pastors. Still, he had a great positive influence on me that remains to this day! He is one of the kindest persons I know. His enthusiasm for the things of God is contagious. But more than anything else, his simple faith in the power and integrity of God's Word has been an inspiration to and impetus for my own faith in God. Thank you Pastor Joe for showing me that nothing is too difficult for God. Encouraged by your example, I know that I will continue to excel in Christ.

Saving the Best for Last

June 23, 1990 is a date that has become indelibly imprinted in my memory. That is the day that I entered into marital covenant with the lovely Kimberly Salyce Pinkney. Kimberly, since the day that we married, has truly proven to be a consistent and very capable helpmeet to me. I believe that she is the greatest human being that I have ever encountered in all my life.

She is the person that knows the most about me. She knows things about me that I would not dare share in any book. And yet she is the person who is most accepting of me. Incidentally, she is also the person whose company I most prefer. She encourages me to follow the dreams that God has placed in my heart, and she offers her love and support every step of the way. She simply brings out the best in me. Without her, I might be writing a book of a different kind. Without her, my story would surely be incomplete.

Thank you Baby for seeing in me what no one else could see—what even I could not see. When I struggled with my own masculinity, you were there to encourage and re-assure me. When other people ridiculed me for my feminine mannerisms, you decidedly looked beyond those mannerisms to see the real me. Thank you for all the times you walked with me unashamedly, hand in hand, through crowded streets, shopping centers, restaurants and at company picnics. Your powerful presence at my side was an unmistakable signal to everyone that I was not the person they believed me to be, but rather that I was God's handiwork. God's man!

My years of freedom from homosexuality have been wonderful but sometimes difficult. I am convinced that without you, they would have been even more difficult. God has used you to affect in me the greatest and most rewarding personal changes that I have ever experienced in my life. Thank you for being a woman that God could use to express Himself to me in a greater and more lasting way. Most of all, I thank you for always being here for me.

Proverbs 31:10 begins with the following questions: "Who can find a virtuous woman?" With confidence and without hesitation, I believe that I can answer that question. And my answer would be: *I can! In fact, I have found a virtuous woman.* You are that virtuous woman! Thank you! I appreciate you! I love you and am excited about spending the rest of my life with you.

There are many more people that I could thank, but this book is simply not large enough. For those of you who have encouraged my family and me in any way (and you know who you are!), I thank you from the bottom of my heart. May God bless you in the way that you have been a blessing to me. I am particularly grateful for the men God has placed in my paths, mainly during my tenure at Now Faith who, by their strong show of manhood, were powerful and positive examples for me. Thank you, Pastor Ray Whittington, Pastor Terry Thomas, Brother Johnny Young, Brother Arthur Knight, Brother Elijah Hawkins, Brother José Sayan, Brother Stephen Koch, Brother John Fisher and Brother Joseph Johnson. You have impacted me more than you will ever know!

About the Authors

The Pinkneys believe that they have been called of God to help people overcome bondage God's way and experience constant victory in their everyday lives. The Pinkneys are currently clearing their schedules and preparing for full time ministry. In particular, they are planning to launch a series of *Grace and Truth* conferences where they will promote the Biblical perspective of homosexuality, which expresses the tireless mercy of God while maintaining the integrity of the Word of God.

When Robert and Kimberly Pinkney met and married, they realized that they had much in common. Both had spent a great part of their lives under demonic control. Robert had battled homosexuality, low self-esteem and suicidal thoughts. Kimberly had been plagued with a variety of sicknesses and tormenting thoughts. Both however had been finally brought to peace and triumph through the delivering power of God. They knew that one day God would call upon them to share their stories so that other people could be free as well. This message will empower the Christian and non-Christian to come out of any satanic bondage. In essence, the book fulfills Luke 4:18, 19: "The

Spirit of the Lord is upon me because He hath anointed me to preach the gospel to the poor; He hath sent me to heal the brokenhearted, to preach deliverance to the captives, and recovering of sight to the blind, to set at liberty them that are bruised, to preach the acceptable year of the Lord." Robert and Kimberly sincerely hope that every person reading this book will understand that regardless of the closet of sin in which you cower, the Word of God is the key to unlocking the door to your deliverance and bringing you forever into His marvelous love.

www.ingramcontent.com/pod-product-compliance
Lightning Source LLC
Chambersburg PA
CBHW051759040426
42446CB00007B/435